WHAT OTHERS ARE SAYING
ABOUT THIS BOOK:

"If you're single and looking for a partner—for dance or for life, read this book. Craig Marcott makes it simple by removing a lot of the guesswork."
> —Annie Hirsch, Director of the
> World Swing Dance Council

"In his new book, *Three Minutes of Intimacy*, Craig Marcott advocates dance as an enhancement to social success. His thesis is compelling. Social dance *can* make you irresistible to the opposite sex."
> —Michael Fitzmaurice,
> Publisher of *Dancing USA*

"Have you ever watched another couple dancing and thought, 'I wish I could do that'? . . . but you don't have a partner, and . . . well, you don't know how to dance? Now you can have it all. Craig Marcott has laid out a simple, easy way to dance your way to a new social life. This book removes all the guesswork that stands between you and what you have always wanted to do. Buy it, read it, and change your life!"
> —John Wheaton,
> Professional dance instructor and
> member of the board of directors of
> the World Swing Dance Council

Three Minutes of Intimacy

Dance Your Way to a Sensational Social Life

Craig Marcott

Sundance Publishing, Inc.
Patchogue, NY

Sundance Publishing Inc.
Post Office Box 932
Patchogue, NY 11772-0932, U.S.A
http://www.Sundancepublishing.net

First Printing 2000

Cover Illustration ©2000 by Rhonda Polen Wernick
Cover and Interior Design by Lightbourne

Library of Congress Cataloging-in-Publication Data
(Provided by Quality Books, Inc.)

Marcott, Craig.
    Three minutes of intimacy : dance your way to a
sensational social life / Craig Marcott. -- 1st ed.
    p. cm.
    LCCN: 00-90827
    ISBN: 0-9678701-2-7

    1. Dance--Social aspects. 2. Interpersonal
relations. I. Title.

GV1595.M37 2000   793.3
          QB100-437

DEDICATION

In memory of Rene and Rita Marcott

To my father, who taught me that the only
true failure is in not making the attempt

and

to my mother, who epitomized
grace in life and courage in death.

Thank you both for walking the walk.

ACKNOWLEDGMENTS

Writing this book has been a journey that could not have been completed without the help of my dance colleagues at Swing Dance Long Island, whose insight and anecdotes made this work possible.

Many dance professionals also contributed significantly to this project. Margaret Batiuchok started me on my way to becoming a desirable dance partner by instilling the requisite fundamentals. Paul and Carol Grecki continued the process, with Paul providing valuable insight into the instructor's viewpoint. Dance professionals Larry Schulz, Patti Panebianco, and Sherry Palencia contributed their East Coast experience.

Special thanks go to Annie Hirsch, Skippy Blair, and her extremely capable assistant, Carl, all of whom gave me a great deal of support and encouragement in my endeavor. They provided invaluable information on the latest trends occurring in social dance around the world.

Norfleet Jones and his shagger colleagues gave me the low-down on Carolina shag. The editors and publishers of the numerous dance magazines were a tremendous source of help and advice. Editors Chris Roerdon and Teddy Kempster made this into a publishable work. A very special thanks goes to Patti Johnson, who was not only a significant part of the editing process, but also a constant source of encouragement. She knew when and where to give me that necessary kick to get me to the next stage.

Most of all, I would like to thank my family and friends, all of whom were so supportive of this project, from beginning to end. My sister, Suzanne, deserves special credit for tolerating—with her usual good humor—all of the insecurities that surfaced during the writing process.

DISCLAIMER

This book is designed to provide information with regard to the subject matter covered. It is sold with the understanding that neither the publisher nor the author intends the reader to engage in any physical activity that can be construed as out of the ordinary. There is no intent by the publisher and author to cause the reader to unduly exert or strain himself physically. Partner dancing is considered by the publisher and author to be well within the realm of ordinary and normal movement for a healthy human. A healthy human being has no physical problems concerning motor skills, or the use of joints or muscles. Should you experience any pain from any movement in general or with regard to partner dancing, you should seek the advice of your physician before continuing. Do not exceed any limitations your physician suggests.

This book contains information with regard to dance contracts and dance studios which is meant to be used as a guideline only. This book is sold with the understanding that the publisher and authors are not engaged in rendering legal or other professional services.

Three Minutes of Intimacy does not guarantee that you will find a life partner. No such guarantee exists. This book was written on the premise that partner dancing can enhance your social life. Learning how to partner dance requires your commitment of time, effort, and money.

Every effort has been made to make this manual as complete within its scope and as accurate as possible. However, there may be mistakes, both typographical and in content. Therefore, this text should be used only as a general guide and not as the ultimate source of dance information.

The purpose of this text is to educate and entertain. The

CONTENTS

1 TWO TO TANGO

If you cannot get rid of the family skeleton, you may as well make it dance.

—George Bernard Shaw

Some people claim that dancing is a reflection of life. Others say that dance is life. A friend of mine once described himself as a cerebral dancer. When I asked him what he meant, he replied that while listening to music he would often dance to it—in his mind. He only wished that he could, in reality, lead his wife—who loved to dance—in a tango or fox trot. The two of them occasionally danced around the house, but it was never truly partner dancing, since he did not know the steps.

It is my hope that after reading this book, those of you who have been cerebral dancers will take the next step—so to speak—and transform your dreams and desires into something real and permanent. Men will find that knowing how to dance will boost their confidence, making it easier to meet women. Women will enjoy the feeling of dancing in the arms of a man. Dancing is a passion, and it is a fact that people who have cultivated varied passions such as dance generally experience more fun and enjoyment in their lives.

The sharing of body movements to music, performed with a leader and follower, creates an unparalleled three minutes of intimacy with another human being. These three minutes, and how they can lead to relationships of all kinds, are the central theme of this endeavor. Relationships, as virtually everyone will acknowledge, are important to our mental well-being. We derive immense meaning from giving and receiving, from loving and being loved. Dance provides the opportunity to develop relationships where both men and women can experience happiness. Happiness is—and I believe we will all agree on this—a worthy pursuit.

> **There are many bright, intelligent, and interesting people sitting at home rather than out socializing because they are too worn down to continue their search for the love, affection, and physical contact they need and desire.**

There are short-cuts to happiness, and dancing is one of them.
—Vicki Baum, *I Know What I'm Worth* (1964)

"That was great!" remarked Diane. "I'm so glad you talked me into coming that night I called you. This beats the singles bars any day. The atmosphere is much more comfortable, and everyone is so friendly! Someone already invited me to go to another dance on Thursday. I never imagined it would be this easy!"

Diane had previously called to inquire about a series of evening dance workshops our club was sponsoring. She had been very ambivalent about venturing out alone, at night, to a dance workshop without a partner.

I knew exactly what she was feeling. In response to an advertisement promoting swing dance, I had walked into the Driftwood Inn on a cold, wintry night almost three years earlier, discouraged and lonely, looking for something to ameliorate the emptiness. Never did I dream of the passion, the fun, and, especially, the incredible social life that awaited me.

There are many bright, intelligent, and interesting people sitting at home rather than out socializing because they are too worn down to continue their search for the love, affection, and physical contact they need and desire. Social dancing, also known as partner-style dancing, partner dancing, and "touch dancing," is a terrific remedy for this situation. It builds confidence instead of destroying it. As you become more skilled, you become more sure of yourself. And from the moment you walk onto the dance floor with a partner, there is the physical contact. It is comforting, often exciting and stimulating, even sensuous. It really is a perfect way to begin a relationship. Both partners are doing something that they enjoy, thereby making conversation relatively easy. Conversation can, in turn, lead to a more friendly chat over a cup of coffee, to dinner (and dancing, of course), and eventually, if things work out, romance. Or it may lead to a friendship and an expanded circle of acquaintances, which may in turn lead to a more intimate relationship.

Men and women come to dance with different expectations.

Men and women come to dance with different expectations. This should not be a surprise to most of us. Leil Lowndes, in her bestseller, *How to Make Anyone Fall in Love with You,* points out many of the different attitudes between men and women. The vast majority of men, for instance, are not about to give up Monday night football for the love of music or the art of dance. They are interested in meeting women and in a sexual encounter. If learning how to dance will increase their chances in achieving those goals, they will, under the right circumstances, invest the time required to learn.

Women are likewise interested in meeting persons of the

opposite sex (POS). However, their interests tend to be geared more toward relationships and dance. A study of 500 female dancers between the ages of 25 and 45, single and married, shows that, in order of importance, dance comes first, followed by financial success and then sex. This would explain why, when Clark Gable walked into the Savoy (a popular New York dance hall in the heyday of Lindy Hop) and someone shouted, "Hey, Clark Gable's in the house!" the reply that followed was, "Oh yeah, can he dance?"

> **Herein lies just one of the differences between the sexes. Men usually resist females intruding on their perceived territory. Women invite guys to come and play on their turf.**

That women find the ability to partner dance so attractive may explain why they never ask me why I swing dance. Dancing is so natural to many women that they can't understand why anyone *wouldn't* want to dance. It's sort of like men and sports. Can you imagine one man asking another, "Why do you like to play softball?" Doesn't happen. Wouldn't happen. But a man might, if he were willing to risk a cold stare provoked by his political incorrectness, ask a softball-playing woman why *she* did so. Herein lies just one of the differences between the sexes. Men usually resist females intruding on their perceived territory. Women invite guys to come and play on their turf.

I social dance and enjoy it just as I enjoy any other sport such as skiing and tennis. I enjoy having a woman in my arms as we gracefully move around the dance floor together. And now that I've become a reasonably good dancer, I like it that women often ask me to dance. Before, I had to do the asking. And I often got rejected. That rarely happens now. I enjoy my newfound popularity with the opposite sex and the opportunities it affords to build new relationships.

Women seem to understand it when I mention relationships. Men don't. When a man asks me the reason I dance, I keep the answer short and sweet: "Because that's where the girls are." *That* they understand.

The social interaction surrounding partner dancing results in a constantly expanding network of new friends and activities. For example, my sister has taken up windsurfing through contacts made at dancing, and recently she was given an aerial tour around Manhattan by a member of Swing Dance Long Island who happens to be a pilot. The opportunities to meet people and engage in new experiences are boundless. We started a dinner group in which a few of us dancers get together every month at someone's home. Some of the people eventually brought friends from outside the dance group. You may get invited to play golf or tennis. Or perhaps you'll find some people to go with on a nice dance vacation around Europe. There are all sorts of ways to meet new and interesting people. Dancing can take you well beyond the proverbial wooden floor. How *far* beyond, and how involved you get, is up to you.

> **Dancing can take you well beyond the proverbial wooden floor. How *far* beyond, and how involved you get, is up to you.**

Let us read and let us dance—two amusements that will never do any harm to the world.
   —Voltaire

Don, a friend of mine, has recently recognized the potential of social dancing. He is currently in the unfortunate position of going through a divorce and is wondering how he is going to meet women in his new role as a single 40-something male. Don is handsome, in good physical condition, and financially stable. His job as a computer programmer, however, provides him with limited opportunities to meet POS. Don remembered that I was working on this book and called me for more information about social dancing. Afterwards, Don concluded that dancing could provide a way for him to ease some of the loneliness while enjoying social and physical contact with women.

It was this conversation that made me realize there is constant turnover in the singles market. I knew from experience that it isn't unusual for dancers to meet a future life partner on the dance floor, but it hadn't occurred to me that there is a constant influx of new people resulting from divorce. We don't like to think about this possibility, but for many people it is a part of life, and they are unexpectedly thrown into a situation that is unfamiliar to them. Don's interest in social dance as a way to meet and enjoy the company of women was particularly interesting. It shows that there are single men who are lonely, but don't want to go to singles bars. Contrary to popular belief, being a single man does not automatically mean you have it made.

For single men who have eschewed the singles marketplaces for whatever reason(s), touch dancing is a great way to have fun, get exercise, and meet women (I'll leave it to you to place these benefits in order of importance). For single women, social dancing is a terrific way to meet those men who have chosen to stay away from the typical singles scene. It is not unreasonable to believe that the type of men who are willing to make the commitment to learn how to partner dance—not to mention return week after week—are more likely to commit to a relationship.

Social dancing also gets you away from the numbers game recommended by some of the books on dating. The game—and it *is* a game—is based upon one of the foundational precepts of sales—the proverbial "cold call." You are supposed to walk up to a total stranger, introduce yourself, and initiate a conversation. This is an intimidating proposition for many people, and becomes even more so after a number of rejections. Rejection in sales is rarely personal; rejection in romance is always personal. It takes a person with inordinate self-confidence to slough off rejection and keep on trying. Even someone with the thickest of skins will eventually wither under the stress if enough rejection occurs.

> **... partner dancing is a great way of getting to know somebody, "because you are forced into an intimate situation and you have to rely on each other."**

Partner dancing eliminates the negative aspects of the numbers game. There is no "cold call." No initial conversation is required except to request a dance, or accept the offer. You immediately have something to talk about—dancing—if you so choose. If talking interferes with your ability to lead or keep the rhythm, smile. And you have the physical contact. How many conversations would you have to initiate, how many offers to get together for a drink or a cup of coffee, how many false starts, and how many rejections would you have to suffer before you could hope to be held in someone's arms? Partner dancing offers you that opportunity the minute you step on the dance floor.

If you have trouble meeting members of the opposite sex, partner dancing is an easy entrée to other active people who are interested in socializing and building relationships. Actress Julia Roberts claims that social or partner dancing is a great way of getting to know somebody, "because you are forced into an intimate situation and you have to rely on each other."

Partner dancing is sensual, but safe. You're holding one another while enjoying the music. It's easier to initiate an intimate relationship when you're touching someone, as opposed to freestyle dancing where you're both gyrating your bodies independently to the often deafening sounds fomented by the disco deejay. Yet there are rules, and I think those of us who are looking for a relationship take a certain comfort in that, especially in today's society. We know who's supposed to lead and who's supposed to follow. There are rules of etiquette which, as in golf or tennis, are expected to be adhered to. When you ask someone to dance, or accept an invitation to dance, there are no other expectations or implications. Just three minutes on the dance floor. Three intimate minutes, to be sure. But once the dance is over, you're free to move on, needing only to follow basic manners and courtesy.

We are also introduced to people whom we wouldn't ordinarily get to meet. For instance, at our dance club, quite a few of the male members are from nearby Brookhaven National Laboratories, so there are more than the expected number of physicists *cutting a rug* (swing dance jargon which simply means "dancing" or "swing dancing"). There are also doctors, teachers, real estate agents, managers, artists, entrepreneurs, musicians, lawyers, and, of course, writers. Where else would you be able to meet such a hodgepodge of people, male and female, in one room, on a regular basis and actually have an opportunity to converse with them? Or better yet, dance with them?

Dancing is the key, or at least one of the keys, to health and happiness. You do not even have to be a good dancer to realize the benefits of this great sport. If you're a man and know the basic footwork and technique required to lead your partner around the dance floor, that's enough. A woman who is capable of following a man's lead can dance with most partners. There are reasons to work on your technique, to improve your dancing ability, which I will explore more deeply later. The bottom line is that you don't have to be a

Fred Astaire or Ginger Rogers to enjoy dance.

Partner-style dancing sometimes seems to pose a threat to the male ego. This concern is not shared by Latino men, however, who consider dancing to be macho. While it is not certain how this difference in attitude developed, we do know that the tango was a popular form of entertainment for Argentine cowboys when they returned from their cattle drives. Women were relatively scarce, competition for their attention fierce, and it was therefore only logical that the better male dancers had more opportunities for female companionship. It may therefore have been a matter of Darwinian survival that led to this cultural difference. There are, however, increasing numbers of American men who are learning the aphrodisiac qualities of partner dancing.

In addition to being adventurous and a fun night on the town, social dancing is great exercise. It gets the heart pumping and burns calories as well. Dancesport, which is the competitive version of ballroom dancing, requires as much training as any other sport. In England, competitive ballroom dancing is covered in the sport section of *The Times* of London.

Social dancing is even making its way into health clubs, which see it as both a form of exercise and a way to add greater dimension to their facility. People who go to health clubs are often interested in both physical fitness and social interaction. Partner dancing addresses both aspects, helping bodies become better balanced and more supple, while simultaneously providing members with a more active social life.

Some people even use social dancing to help focus their attention away from serious illnesses. One man went so far as to schedule his amateur dance competitions around chemotherapy treatments. Others have used forms of social dance as a visualization tool to stimulate their immune system. On a less esoteric level, touch dancing can provide a sanctuary or refuge during those difficult times which we all face occasionally in our lives.

This is not the kind of partner dancing you saw your parents do at your cousin's wedding.

Social dancing encompasses many different types of dancing, each having its own distinctive style. The Lindy Hop, or Lindy, is the "granddaddy" of all the swing dances, having given birth to East Coast Swing, West Coast Swing, Carolina Shag, St. Louis Shag, jitterbug, boogie-woogie (Germany), jive (England) and others. The Lindy is red hot right now, with the younger generation adding aerial steps from the past into their dance routines for even greater excitement. This is not the kind of partner dancing you saw your parents do at your cousin's wedding. Those of us who are in the baby boomer stage usually refrain from these higher levels of adventure, but as the Duke Ellington song says, "It don't mean a thing if it ain't got that swing!"

"Ballroom style" dance is also a major form of social dance and includes incredibly sexy dances such as salsa and tango. The popularity of these dances is reflected in the abundance of dance-related movies, such as *Strictly Ballroom, Shall We Dance?, Swing Kids,* and, more recently, *Dance With Me.* Ballroom dancing has become very popular on many student campuses, with thousands of college students enrolling in dance organizations and classes.

All partner-style dances incorporate both social and sexual elements, although the balance of each varies. Contra dancing, for instance, is extremely social—it is not uncommon to see entire families participating. On the other hand, West Coast Swing, the official state dance of California, is recognized for both its gracefulness and sensuality.

Dance, v.i. To leap about to the sound of tittering music, preferably with arms about your neighbor's wife or daughter. There are many kinds of dances, but all those requiring the participation of the two sexes have two characteristics in common: they are conspicuously innocent, and warmly loved by the vicious.

—*The Devil's Dictionary*

There is one important difference between dancing and other sports such as golf or tennis. In dancing, the participants are typically of the opposite sex, and if they are to succeed, they must work together instead of competing with one another. How many other sports can make those claims?

So, is dancing for you? Only you can answer that. First, ask yourself, "Do I have any interest in learning how to dance?" In other words, have you had a yearning to dance before but for some reason failed to act upon it? That is not the same as having no desire to learn. If the latter is true, I suggest you stay away from dancing, just as you avoid any sport you have no interest in.

For me, a lack of interest applies to golf. My father loved the game. He played it most of his life. He woke up at 5 a.m. on the weekends to make tee time. He touted its benefits: exercise, socializing, business, etc. I've tried it, and I just can't get into walking all over creation chasing some obnoxious little ball that absolutely refuses to do my bidding. By the end of the second hole my blood pressure has quadrupled (so much for the health aspect), my own partners have asked to "play through" (so much for socializing), and my temper is at the flash point (good-bye business relationships).

The bottom line is that you can't fake it, not for any length of time, anyway. On the other hand, if you've stayed away from the dance floor because you weren't any good at it but would like to learn, that's a different story. With some lessons and practice, you'll be better than most.

My Uncle Bob is a perfect example of how practice can overcome an absence of talent. He decided to take up golf so he could play on Sundays with my father. Why he suddenly had this urge to get up at 5 a.m. on weekends is beyond me, but everyone has idiosyncrasies, and Uncle Bob had his—the worst golf swing I've ever seen, on or off a fairway. Once he placed a golf club in his hand, he became so awkward and stiff he made Al Gore look like a natural. I figured my uncle would never make it onto a golf course. I was dead wrong. Day after day, Uncle Bob would head out to his backyard and hit golf balls. And then hit more golf balls. After a while, I noticed his swing became smoother, and the ball traveled farther and straighter. Eventually, after hitting countless practice balls, Uncle Bob ventured onto the golf course with my father where he shot under a hundred. His first golf game!

Take my word for it, you have more dance talent than my uncle has golf talent. I guarantee it. If you didn't, you couldn't walk straight. So you can *do* this. It's a question of desire. How badly do you want to dance? How important is it for you to have a great social life? These are questions only you can answer.

If you can walk you can dance. If you can talk you can sing.
—Zimbabwe Proverb

You don't have to be a natural to learn how to dance. Frankie Manning, one of the originators of the Lindy Hop, likes to tell the story about the time his mother took him to one of the dance clubs in New York. Frankie was just twelve years old at the time, but at the end of the night his mother told him, "Frankie, one thing's for sure. You're never going to be a dancer. You're just too stiff." Most of us wish we were as "stiff" as Frankie Manning. That would be like saying we wish we were as "awkward" as Fred Astaire. Frankie was a top competitor in the 1940s when the popularity of Lindy Hop was at its zenith. Today he travels around the world teaching the style of Lindy he helped develop. Few of us have that kind of talent or will develop it to that level. The good news is that we don't have to. Just knowing *how* to dance will put you one up on most of the people out there.

You may now be saying to yourself, "Okay, this sounds pretty good. I don't need a partner and I don't need to have the talent of a Fred Astaire or Ginger Rogers to make this thing work. So what's the catch?"

Well, you've got to be willing to invest some of your time. This book is not only about dancing, but about building relationships through dance. And that doesn't happen in one night. Remember, nothing good comes without effort. But in this case, the fun is in the journey.

If you've always wanted to learn how to dance, or know how but haven't been able to parlay it into a better social life, you couldn't have chosen a better time to pick up this book. A whole new world can open for you.

All the ills of mankind, all the tragic misfortunes that fill the history books, all the political blunders, all the failures of the great leaders have arisen merely from a lack of skill at dancing.
—Moliere

2 THE ULTIMATE CONNECTION

Dancing is wonderful training for girls, it's the first way you learn to guess what a man is going to do before he does it.

—Christopher Morley

Social dancing offers an introduction to another person which is extraordinary in terms of physical intimacy. When you're in direct contact with your partner, you're able to get a sense of how he or she moves. Is he gentle or rough, forceful or timid, persuasive or unsure? Does she follow well or does she want to lead? This physical connection between dancers can be overpowering, with the leader forcefully directing his partner to the intended position, or it can be as subtle as a slight bit of tension between their fingertips. As one dance instructor put it, "a little tension can be a good thing."

My sister, Suzanne, feels that someone's dance personality gives a very good indication of his or her true personality in the real world. If her male partner tends to be pushy, aggressive, or overly forceful on the dance floor, he is likely to have similar characteristics off the floor. Other personality traits, such as shyness, nervousness, and conviviality seem to be conveyed through dance as well. My personality trait "antennae" are not as finely tuned as my sister's (and, it would seem, most women's), but I agree with her position in general, adding only that in my opinion it is easier to discern these traits when dancing with an experienced partner. In other words, as people become better dancers and, therefore, more comfortable with their environment and more confident in their ability, the more likely they will express their true nature on the "wood." It is also less likely that their partners will interpret their initial feelings of nervousness and awkwardness as a personality trait, but rather as symptoms commonly associated with the learning stages of dance.

. . . someone's dance personality gives a very good indication of his or her true personality in the real world. If her male partner tends to be pushy, aggressive, or overly forceful on the dance floor, he is likely to have similar characteristics off the floor.

The truest expression of a people is in its dances and its music. Bodies never lie.
—Agnes DeMille

Your proximity to your dance partner provides you with the opportunity for verbal dialogue as well, so you can establish a conversational relationship in addition to a physical one.

One of the things that social dancing undeniably provides is an alternative to the bar scene. Many ladies come to check out our dances, then come back the following week with one or more of their friends because they find the atmosphere "so comfortable and friendly," allowing people to move at a more leisurely pace in developing relationships. By the way, relationships are the key to the success of partner-style dancing as a social form. Have you ever gone to a singles bar only to return home without having spoken to anyone except the bartender? It doesn't exactly encourage you to go out again.

Many women complain about the quality of men they meet at bars and other singles events. However, if you stop to think about it, this problem shouldn't come as a surprise. The men who are successful in this type of environment are "experts." They have honed the skills required to meet women in these situations. The fact that they have become proficient at "picking up" women usually makes them less-than-ideal partners for any type of long-term relationship. They usually have their choice of women. When a problem pops up, it is easier for them to find another woman than to stick around and try to resolve the issue.

A corollary of the typical singles situation is that these experts are actively searching the room for the most attractive women. Unlike most men, who become nervous just entertaining the thought of approaching such a woman, these smooth operators thrive on pick-ups. That means that a woman must expect to be judged exclusively on her looks.

You can't lie when you dance. It's so direct. You do what is in you. You can't dance out of the side of your mouth.
—Shirley MacLaine, *Shirley and Warren,* by James Spada

The men you meet at social dances tend to be of different quality. These are the men who are uncomfortable in the bar scene and many other singles events. Unless you happen to meet a man at work or bump into one at the supermarket, such men aren't easy to find (a fact which I'm sure comes as no surprise to many of you ladies). One of the best places to meet such men are at social dances. Men who attend these events have usually made a commitment to learn how to dance, so the chances of them returning week after week are pretty good. They are also less likely to smoke and drink, since these activities are often not permitted at dances.

Women often claim that the men involved in "touch" dancing tend to be more romantic. One reason could be that these men are more likely to appreciate any relationships that develop, compared with the "expert" who may tend to take his success for granted.

. . . one of the strongest social benefits of partner-style dancing is its opportunity for networking.

In the bar scene, each new prospect is a total unknown, and the process of introduction not only must occur on an individual basis, but must be repeated constantly and relentlessly to be effective. In contrast, one of the strongest social benefits of partner-style dancing is its opportunity for networking, so let's take a look at how this works.

I've never been enamored of the term *networking*, perhaps because it sounds too much like *working*. What we're really talking about is the building of relationships, a very natural process. Take the following example:

Debbie goes to a weekly social dance. Week after week she dances with a variety of men and over some period of time gets involved in more friendly and intimate conversation with some of them. Friendships develop (in this example we're going to assume that nothing romantic exists in these relationships) and eventually Debbie begins to get invitations to some of the other social or sports-related activities these men are involved in, such as skiing, bowling, windsurfing, golf, and so on. At these activities she meets other people and eventually does get involved in a romantic relationship. What part of this activity was work? Debbie got involved only in the activities she wanted to get involved in, and with the people she wanted to be involved with! The friendships that led to these invitations could just as well have been with women, with the same result. And even if no romantic relationship had developed, Debbie has a multitude of new friends and hobbies and a heck of a social life. Better than her sitting home on Saturday night wondering what she's going to do other than wash her hair, isn't it?

I should warn you that once someone begins to experience the benefits of partner dancing, it often leads to addiction (a relatively harmless one, unless you happen to be married and going out every night without your spouse, something I personally don't recommend).

Once someone gets involved with one type of social dancing, he or she often begins to experiment with other styles of dance. It's like eating potato chips—almost impossible to stop with just one. Before you know it, you'll be dancing Lindy Hop on Monday, West Coast Swing on Tuesday, country western on Wednesday, then taking a day off to rest your weary body before hitting the ballroom floor for a hot salsa on Friday.

One of the terrific things about dancing is its ability to raise the spirits. My friend Kathy calls it a "runner's high." That's the feeling she gets after one or two dances. Even if she's in a depressed mood, she'll go dancing because she knows that after the first dance her mood will improve. She's not looking for romance, although she acknowledges that it could happen. But there's no doubt about the *esprit de corps* that's developed between Kathy and her dance friends since she took to the wooden floor. "My social life is better than it's ever been thanks to dancing. I've met new people and we make plans to go out or have dinner. It's just as likely I'll meet someone through all of the friendships and contacts that I've made from dancing as I will on the dance floor."

Although there are benefits to single life, those of us who

fall into this category are all too aware of the potential pitfalls and disadvantages associated with our lifestyle. It is too easy to choose to stay at home and find something to occupy our time rather than go out into a world of strangers and the unknown. This is especially true if our destination is without purpose. Social dancing changes that. Once you get started, chances are you will become hooked on it like the rest of us. Your neighbors will begin to wonder where you go every night (especially, ladies, if you wear short skirts). Your children, if you have any, will think they are orphans. Your non-dancing friends may wonder if you have gone over the edge.

> **Dancing is not a seasonal sport. You can do it any time, year-round, which makes it ideal no matter where you live or what the climate.**

One of our female members skis in the winter and sails competitively as a member of a yacht club during the warmer months. She started coming to our dances about a year ago and now says that if she were forced to choose one sport, it would be dancing. She claims dancing has improved her agility and endurance, and is the only sport she's aware of in which women can participate with men and yet not be competitive with them. "You're actually partners out there on the dance floor, so you have to work together." She laughed. "Of course, I still don't follow as well as I could, so that frustrates them a little." As I said earlier, a little tension can be a good thing.

Dancing is not a seasonal sport. You can do it any time, year-round, which makes it ideal no matter where you live or what the climate. You don't have to worry about dressing for the weather, putting on gloves and boots and other paraphernalia that you need for winter sports like ice skating and downhill and cross-country skiing. A person doesn't require any special gear or clothing except maybe a pair of good dance shoes.

Social dancing can also make travel even more enjoyable. Many dancers, when planning a vacation or business trip, check to see what dance venues are available at their destinations. This makes vacations more fun by adding another option for evening entertainment, and offers those people who travel for business purposes an alternative to a boring or lonely night in a motel room. If you are really serious about your dancing, there are many companies that orchestrate dance vacations. Some of these vacations have included European tours, where swing dancing is extremely popular. I have included a list of U.S. dance organizations in the *Resource Guide* in the back of this book. Additional information can be found by accessing the Internet.

Anna, another of our members, sums up her reasons for partner-style dancing as follows: "Number one, I love the music. I can internalize it and then express it through rhythm. Secondly, I love the physical connection with my partner. It allows me to experience a spontaneous harmony as we share the same thing. There is a value in connecting that you don't find in disco dancing. And lastly, I enjoy the socializing."

So if you find your feet tapping the floor when you listen to music and you're looking for some fun and a little physical contact on the dance floor, read on and I'll share with you how to get started. This is exciting! Your time has finally arrived. Be adventurous and dance your way to a better social life!

The nature of my compulsion was such that I danced in my sleep. The entire household was sometimes awakened by loud thumping sounds coming from my room.
　　　　—Gelsey Kirkland,
　　　　　Dancing on My Grave (1986)

3 WHY MEN DON'T DANCE . . . AND WHY THEY SHOULD!

*Dancing is an **amazing** activity. You can go up to a gorgeous woman that you've never met before, spend three minutes touching her virtually any-where on her body, and she **thanks** you for it afterward!*
—Mario Robau, Jr., champion dance instructor, interjecting some humor at a workshop in Bethesda, MD

To my female readers: It has been my experience that men require more persuasion than women before they decide they are willing to attempt partner-style dancing. Once they experience the benefits of this type of dance, they are much more likely to continue with it. The purpose of this chapter is to make men aware of those benefits so they will want to learn these dances and join you on the dance floor. If so, it will mean additional partners for you. Perhaps you can use the material in this chapter to convince some of your male friends to join in the fun.

One of our female dance members lamented, "I don't understand why it's so difficult to get guys to learn how to dance. In today's society where it's politically incorrect for a man to express too much masculinity, the dance floor is one of the few places left where it's okay for the man to be totally dom-inant. He gets to lead and the woman has to follow. And as a woman, that's the way I prefer it, at least on the dance floor."

I've had the opportunity to set up and observe quite a few dance workshops and have spoken with a number of dance instructors as to why, with all the obvious incentives to learn how to dance, many men don't stick with it. I'm convinced that some men quit early in the game because they can't stand the competition. The thought that a woman is progressing faster than he is goes against every grain of his male ego.

> **"In today's society where it's politically incorrect for a man to express too much masculinity, the dance floor is one of the few places left where it's okay for the man to be totally dominant. He gets to lead and the woman has to follow. And as a woman, that's the way I prefer it, at least on the dance floor."**

Paul Grecki, a professional dance instructor and the 1995 American Swing Dance Lindy Hop champion, offers some additional insight.

"Men start at a disadvantage. They are unfamiliar with dancing. They don't know what it's about and so they don't know how to behave.

"Men are afraid of appearing feminine. They believe that real men don't dance. Nothing is further from the truth. The reality is that men who *can* dance have greater access to women than most of the men who don't dance. (As I mentioned in the first chapter, Latino men realize this and consider dancing macho.)

"Men don't want to feel embarrassed in front of the ladies. We don't want to look incompetent in front of women, so we don't want to go to the edge; we don't want to lose control. But it's okay to let loose and have fun. And you are going to experience something much, much more than you'll experience if you go to a bar and just talk to a woman.

You're going to be able to communicate with somebody on another level beside pick-up lines. Dance is like any other sport while you are learning it, but once learned, dance will give you control."

The man who can't dance thinks the band is no good.

—Polish proverb

Paul's point that men start out at a disadvantage because they are unfamiliar with dancing is an excellent one and deserves additional comment. We all

The reality is that men who *can* dance have greater access to women than most of the men who don't dance.

have an innate feeling of music from the beginning of life. All you have to do is watch any child—boy boy or girl—dance uninhibitedly to music to see the truth in this.

As we get older, girls hone their dancing skills while boys gravitate toward other sports. The abundance of soccer moms may represent a change in this scenario, but I'm referring to the current generation of men and women who, for the most part, grew up with fewer opportunities for female sport activities. This divergence in activities leads to awkwardness on the male's part regarding the sport of dance.

I can still remember the high school gym classes where, twice a year, we were lined up according to height, short to tall—I was always third in line—then paired off with our female "height-adjusted equal," and for a full 45 minutes were taught the art of social dancing. Why not have placed us on a stage in front of a hundred of our peers and asked us to give an impromptu speech on the mating habits of the unicorn? We (boys) certainly would have felt less foolish. In retrospect, it would be hard to think of a better way to instill a terminal distaste for partner dancing than the way many boys are introduced to it. The result was that we denigrated it.

"Dancing was for girls, not boys." Boys played football, base-ball, and other manly games. Real boys didn't dance. What we

didn't realize is that real men, and espe-cially socially successful men, do.

". . . dance will give you control."

When a man does decide to attempt to learn how to social dance, he is at a distinct disadvantage. Not only is he unfamiliar with the rhythm and footwork, he must learn how to lead. A woman who is familiar with rhythm and foot-work can follow the leader in most social dances. In contrast, the man must know where he is going on the dance floor, as well as how to direct his partner there. This ostensible unfair-ness between the two roles is eventually equalized by the necessity of the follower to respond, at a split-second notice, to her partner's lead. In the meantime, however, this early obstacle quickly eliminates the men who are not serious about learning how to partner dance. Obstacles, however, offer opportunity—at least for those who persevere. The man who understands that rhythm is an acquired skill, just as learning how to hit a tennis serve or ski down a mountain, understands that learning to dance is merely a matter of practice and repetition. The man who realizes that, and understands that women don't expect perfection, can put his ego aside long enough to learn the physical skills necessary to be successful on the dance floor.

Dancing, specifically partner dancing, may well be the single most effective way to meet women. Arthur Murray used to promote his dance instructions with the catch phrase, "How I Became Popular Overnight!"

In nearly every book on dating, dancing is listed as one of the best ways to meet the opposite sex. Some even refer to it as the "golden key" to meeting women. Why?

Most women love to dance. How often have you heard a woman say she wishes her boyfriend knew how to dance, or complain that she can't get her husband to dance with her? How many times have you seen girls dancing with each other because they lacked skilled male partners? Dance is a female-dominated sport! Learn to dance and you will be a welcome asset at special events such as weddings, anniversaries, parties, and singles dances where music and partner dancing is present. You will be an eagerly anticipated guest at regular scheduled dance events in studios, ballrooms, hotels, and barrooms.

Dancing, specifically partner dancing, may well be the single most effective way to meet women.

Dancing is, in fact, the great equalizer. If a man takes the time to become a skilled and confident leader, his presence is appreciated by every lady in the room. **A good dancer does not need to be handsome to be popular.** Similarly, a woman who is a good dancer radiates grace and charm, regardless of whether she is a physical beauty.

This does not mean that you can use dancing to compensate for a complete lack of social skills. You still need to have good manners and be capable of holding up your end of a conversation. What I am saying is that it is your dancing skills that are going to capture the lady's initial attention and hold it. You will not be dependent on having to say something witty right off the bat. If you happen to be witty, all the better, but it's not essential. The ability to dance will give you the time to build a relationship. Remember, the women at the dances you attend are coming back week after week. There is no need to hurry. In fact, they don't want to be hurried, or harried for that matter.

Asking someone to dance is an easy icebreaker. It becomes even easier once other women in the room see you handle yourself well on the dance floor. Women appreciate men who can make them feel good on the "wood." The more skilled you are, the more they will hope that you ask them for a dance. And isn't this a feeling you want in life? Having women wanting you?

> **The ability to dance well adds a dimension of grace and poise to your appearance. This makes you more attractive to women, the same way a woman who dances gracefully appears more attractive to you.**

I have had numerous conversations with female dancers on the subject of a man's appearance, and their response is that when looking for someone to dance with, they are more interested in the man's ability to dance than his looks. For those of you who may have been skimming over this part, I repeat: **Women are more interested in a man's dancing ability than his looks!** Your response might be, "Yeah, sure. That's what they may say, but they don't really mean it" or "That may be true while on the dance floor, but what about off it?" Let's address both of these concerns.

That's what they may say, but they don't really mean it. First, you've got to put your male mind on hold for a second. You've probably heard of the book *Men Are from Mars, Women Are from Venus* by John Gray, Ph.D. Women are not as hooked on looks as men are, fortunately for us. This does not mean, of course, that they can't appreciate good-looking men or aren't attracted to them. This does mean that the quality of your dancing will tend to neutralize that factor. The ability to dance well adds a dimension of grace and poise to your appearance. This makes you more attractive to women, the same way a woman who dances gracefully appears more attractive to you.

I posed the following question to some of the female dancers at our club. "If Tom Cruise were on the dance floor, would you rather dance with him or one of the better dancers in our club?" Their reply: "It would depend on whether he could dance." To some extent they were being flippant. But they also explained that although they would love to date Tom Cruise (assuming he was single), a man's looks, when they were dancing, were not as important as his compatibility with them on the dance floor.

You may be saying to yourself, "Those women are obviously not representative of the female gender." Wrong. The reason I say this is that I know how women—in a dance situation—responded to me before and after I learned to dance. Before I learned to swing dance, I had a difficult time getting a woman to dance with me. I was never overly assertive, hated taking the risk of being rejected, etc. I also knew that in the "looks" department, I'm not the leading man type. I've been mistaken for a professor and a doctor, but to my knowledge no one has ever confused me with Tom Cruise.

I'm reminded of an interview with the CEO of a Fortune 500 company, who was telling a reporter that the company often groomed its best-looking men to be salesmen. When asked what the company did with its less attractive male employees, the CEO, almost without hesitation and with a slight smile, replied that it made them executives. Let's just say that in his particular company I would probably be an *executive*.

After about six months of dancing and with a few lessons thrown in for good measure, I found I no longer had to ask anyone to dance. Instead, the ladies were asking me!

This might sound like a fantasy, but it isn't. I would ask you to think about two things. First, ask yourself how many guys are both exceedingly handsome *and* know how to dance well. I can assure you that the number of people walking around who fit that description is very small indeed.

Second, think of Fred Astaire. Or rather, think of the way

women think of Fred Astaire. I know, the man is dead, but his image and reputation are far from deceased. Here was a man with average looks who captured the hearts of so many women in America that almost every man wished he could be in his place. Why? Because he could dance so spectacularly that women fell in love with him. I can hear you now: "But I'll never be able to come close to dancing like Fred Astaire." The good news is that you don't have to. What you need to know is that there are very few men out there who can dance—period. You don't have to dance like a professional; all you have to do is dance well enough to make a woman feel good on the dance floor, and the word will spread (unless she decides to keep you for herself, which is a problem most men would love to have).

"Can't act. Slightly bald. Can dance a little."
—Anonymous, studio report after
Fred Astaire's first screen test

That may be true while on the dance floor, but what about off it? When I started going to our local swing (Lindy) dance, I noticed a very polite, very average-looking man in his early forties on the dance floor. The reason I noticed Dave was that he was dancing, very nicely, I might add, with an extremely attractive woman. They were clearly two of the better dancers on the floor. I assumed, incorrectly as it turns out, that they were a couple. They just enjoyed dancing with each other.

Shortly thereafter, a new woman, Lisa, began coming to the dance club. Unlike me, she would definitely be in sales in the aforementioned company. Lisa would capture a man's attention even if she stood in the middle of a group of contestants for the Miss America Beauty Pageant. Black curly hair that accented a beautiful face on top of a dancer's body made it not surprising that Dave would quickly show interest and begin giving Lisa dancing instructions. Today, Lisa and Dave are married.

So how did a nice, unassuming guy like Dave capture Lisa's attention and hold it long enough to win her over with his personality? The answer is dancing. Could he have done it some other way? Possibly. But remember, dancing gave Dave both the icebreaker and the opportunity to build a chemistry through dance. And it provided him with the time to build a relationship.

Dancing is also a great confidence builder. Before their engagement, Lisa agreed to accompany me to the wedding of a friend. As usual, the band played one segment of music from the 1940s. Lisa and I left the table and headed to the dance floor with all the other wedding guests. By this time, I had been dancing for about six months. My skill level was probably in the middle of the dance group at the club. I didn't realize how far I had progressed, however, until the dance floor cleared, leaving Lisa and me alone for the remainder of the dance. People approached us throughout the rest of the evening to tell us what great dancers we were. Talk about walking on air! I can still recall the feeling to this day.

After that first dance with Lisa, I probably could have danced with any woman at the wedding. The only resistance I've ever run across after someone has seen me dance is that they're too intimidated to dance with someone "as good" as me. Translation: they're afraid of not being able to keep up and looking silly on the dance floor. If you can't figure out a response to that objection, you have two choices. Go back and retake Conversation 101 or limit yourself to those females who aren't easily intimidated. Either way, you'll be ahead of where you are now.

There are other advantages gained from learning to dance. While dancing with a woman, you have her completely to yourself. No distractions. No other men stopping by to talk to her. She's yours for three minutes. If you want to converse, this is your chance. At the very least, you'll be holding her hand and gently steering her around the room, the space between you dictated by the particular dance. (The tango, by the way, has perhaps the least amount of space between partners of any of the dances. I just thought you might want to know.) The very nature of social dancing requires you to be in physical contact with one another, providing an opportunity to see if there is any chemistry between the two of you. When chemistry does occur, everything seems to fall into place—the music, the rhythm, the balance. Believe me, when it happens, both of you will know it. It is unlike almost anything else you will experience. And if "physical chemistry" isn't occurring, you still get to hold and move a woman.

> **The tango, by the way, has perhaps the least amount of space between partners of any of the dances.**

As you improve and can lead a woman proficiently in a variety of dances, you will experience even more benefits. Here are three.

First, you will rarely have to leave the dance floor because of not being able to do a particular dance. Similarly, you will not be put in a position of feeling uncomfortable asking someone to dance because you don't know how to do it.

The first dance I learned was the Lindy Hop. Since that was the type of music played the majority of time at the club where I danced, not knowing how to dance to the other music provided me with a breather. Later, as I began to attend other dances and social events where the Lindy Hop was not the prominent dance, I found myself confined to the perimeter so often that I eventually began learning other partner-style dances. Of course, now that the women know I can dance to other kinds of music, they come and ask me to dance even if I'm standing on the sidelines. So much for getting a breather! I'm not complaining, however. If a woman wants to dance with me, and I can, I'll dance. I've spent too many years on the sidelines to waste a golden opportunity to dance with a potential life partner.

> . . . dancing provides, among other things, opportunity. The opportunity to meet new people. The opportunity for them to get to know you. *The opportunity to build relationships.*

Second, the more comfortable your dance partner feels, the more time she is likely to spend on the dance floor with you. And the more comfortable you will be asking her on a dance date. Who knows? She may even become a dance partner. But more about that later.

Third, as you continue to improve, your advantages continue to grow. When you reach the point where women feel more graceful while they are dancing with you, the opportunities for socializing and dating are almost limitless. You will not be afraid to ask the most attractive woman to dance. Many women will want to go out with you because of your dancing ability. Large numbers of women have designed their extracurricular lives around dancing. Your dancing skill will make you more desirable to these women.

It should be obvious by now that dancing provides, among other things, opportunity. The opportunity to meet new people. The opportunity for them to get to know you. *The opportunity to build relationships.*

Dancing may be the common denominator, but it certainly isn't the end-all. I've met all kinds of people with all kinds of backgrounds—doctors, physicists, teachers, clerks, and everything in between. I've met people at dances who ski, windsurf, hike, bicycle, enjoy walks on the beach—you name it. You, too, will meet people with different backgrounds and interests if you decide to become involved in the sport of dance. This is your golden opportunity to get involved in activities with the opposite sex. *Don't be confined by the dance floor.* Explore what is beyond it!

To sum up, by learning how to dance you place yourself in that small minority of men who can do something that most women love to do and wish they could find a man to do it with. *You can be that man.* The women are waiting for you. What are you waiting for?

We should consider every day lost in which we do not dance at least once.

—Nietzsche

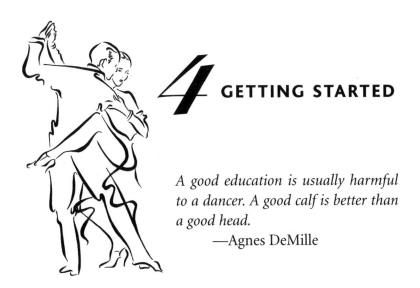

4 GETTING STARTED

*A good education is usually harmful
to a dancer. A good calf is better than
a good head.*
—Agnes DeMille

The first question you may want to ask yourself is, "Why do I want to learn how to dance?" In my case, there were two reasons. First, I had always been fascinated with the Lindy. I liked the music—my foot would begin to tap and my body would begin to move as soon as I heard a song like "In the Mood" or "Blue Suede Shoes"—and I enjoyed watching people who could do the dance well. I wanted to be able to dance like those people.

The second reason was purely social. I wanted to meet persons of the opposite sex (POS). When I saw the advertisement in the Events section of our local newspaper promoting swing dance (no partner needed), I seized the opportunity as a way to achieve both objectives.

If your goal is to learn the basic steps of a few of the more popular dances so you feel more comfortable at weddings and other social situations where dance is part of the occasion, then all you really need do is find an appropriate dance studio (see Chapter 5). If you are interested in using dance to enhance your social life, you may want to consider some of the following:

Music. If it doesn't move you or get your feet moving,

you will find staying with the dance difficult during the early learning stages. Furthermore, it is less likely that the dance will become a lifelong activity if you don't enjoy the music.

This advice is in direct contrast to that given in some dating books, especially those for men, which often recommend that your primary concern should be where to find the greatest number of POS. My opposition to this advice rests on two points. The first is that if you don't like the music, you are not going to enjoy yourself. If you aren't going to have fun with this, you might as well search for romance in the supermarket or laundromat.

My second objection is that if you are fortunate enough to meet someone at a dance and you both hit it off, what happens if you find out he or she has centered her life around that dance? On the other hand, if you begin dancing to music you enjoy, you will have something in common with the people you meet on the dance floor and have a greater chance of building long-term relationships.

Opportunity. Visit nearby dance studios, clubs, and other night spots to get a better feel for the dance and what is available. No matter what type of dance you choose, it is imperative that at minimum there be a weekly dance event so you can practice. I can tell you from hard experience that you will be wasting your money if you don't dance between lessons. In addition, if you aren't able to dance with people on a regular weekly basis you will not have an opportunity to build relationships.

Music is the key to the female heart.
—Johann G. Seume

At one point I decided to take some private cha-cha and fox trot lessons because those were the types of music occasionally played at our dance club to provide a break from the more rigorous demands of swing dancing. I felt that taking private lessons would speed up the learning process, a valid assumption which I discuss later. The problem was that the cha-cha and fox trot were a distinctly minor part of the dance format at our club, providing little opportunity for practice. After about a month of instruction and considerable expense with little to show for it, I gave up.

The moral of this story is that no matter how much you want to learn the mambo, if no weekly mambo dances are available, you aren't going to learn to mambo. If your purpose is to create a better social life for yourself and not just dance around the kitchen with a broom, I suggest finding a dance that is easily accessible to you.

> **If your purpose is to create a better social life for yourself and not just dance around the kitchen with a broom, I suggest finding a dance that is easily accessible to you.**

Life may not be the party we hoped for, but while we're here we should dance.
—Unknown

Proximity. Make sure the dance is within a reasonable driving distance of your home or work so you do not require a superhuman effort to motivate yourself to get out of your house or apartment. Think of it as joining a health club. The closer you are to it, the more likely you are to use it. Dancing is great fun, but there are times when the weather is less than ideal or your time is at a premium. On these occasions, the thought of facing a long drive may be enough to keep you at home instead of enjoying the benefits of dancing. We're only human. When we are tired, it can be difficult to remember how exhilarating it was last week when we were dancing with Bob or Carol. (This is another reason why it is so important to dance at least weekly. The less time between dances, the easier to remember how much fun it was.) Years of observing club members have shown me that the longer the drive, the less likely it is that someone will continue attending the dance.

Atmosphere. If you visit some dance studios and clubs, you will be able to get a "hands on" feel for the music, the dance, and the type of people who attend. Many of the private studios have their own weekly or bi-weekly "social" where students get together for practice. Many of the dance instructors also attend. Since studios use this opportunity to showcase their product, it should be no problem to get an invitation to observe. Dance studios are easy to find; look in the Yellow Pages under "Dance Studios" or "Dancing Instruction."

Night clubs and dance clubs typically have dances on a regular basis; it is merely a matter of finding out where and when so you can stop in and check it out. However, some dance clubs and night spots may not be so easy to locate for the uninitiated. You can start by checking the Yellow Pages under "Night clubs," "Clubs," and "Dance Clubs." Try calling some of these places to see whether they offer dancing, and if so, what kind or style, as well as the age of the average participant. Since ballroom dances can be sponsored by private entities such as deejays, restaurants, night clubs, and dance halls, don't be surprised if you stumble across one or two of these in your investigation.

Another way to find out what type of dance you might be interested in is to experiment with a few through an adult education program at your local school, community college, YMCA, community center or any other local recreation council. Many of these offer short courses that may center on one particular dance or provide a couple of lessons each on a few different dances. Such courses are usually inexpensive and can give you a short introduction to a variety of dances. You also get to meet new people. Some of these programs require that you come with a partner, so make this one of your first questions if you have no one to accompany you.

Often it is the most popular dances that are found at your local bars and restaurants with available floor space. The popularity of various dances tends to be regional and subject to public interest at that particular moment. Lately, the Lindy has become popular throughout the country, especially with the younger crowd. West Coast Swing, tango, and mambo/salsa are also dominant dances in most of the major cities on both coasts. The Carolina Shag is by far the dance of choice throughout most of the Southeast, whereas the St. Louis Shag, Imperial Swing, and West Coast Swing dominate the Midwest.

You probably already know what the popular dances are in your area, but if not, it shouldn't be hard to find out. Just check out the signs on the local night spots as you drive around, or call up a few places that have dancing and ask what they offer during the week. You'll get the picture quickly.

Don't assume that if the dance is in a bar it's the typical bar-scene kind of thing that you're trying to avoid. Partner-style dancing tends to attract its own unique crowd, and that usually excludes those individuals looking for a quick pick-up. As I said before, partner dancing requires some commitment of time and effort, and it very quickly weeds out those who are unwilling to make that commitment.

Also, don't assume that because a certain establishment attracts a particular type of crowd on the weekend it draws the same people during the week. The place where we have our Tuesday night swing dances attracts a totally different type of clientele on Friday and Saturday nights. My sister found this out the hard way. She and a friend decided to check out the situation one Saturday in a bar that featured freestyle dancing and found it representative of everything she hated about the singles scene—too many pick-up lines and not enough decent conversation. Her night abruptly ended when a man she was dancing with leaned over and without warning stuck his tongue in her ear, apparently thinking this approach would stimulate some kind of reaction. He was right. It did. My point is that it's more often the type of dance than the place that determines the crowd.

Ask. When you visit any of these establishments, ask the dancers where they go to dance socially. Many of them are involved in other types of dance, and if you ask them, they should be able to tell you where people go for "such and such" style of dance. Many of the dancers at our club, for instance, are involved in ballroom, country western and West Coast Swing, in addition to the Lindy. If you were to ask, they could tell you where to go for dancing and lessons in all of these styles. Don't be afraid to ask. Dancers love what they do and are eager to get others involved.

Dances such as the Lindy, West Coast Swing, and contra dancing tend to be run by non-profit organizations. Depending on where you live, however, any particular style can be run as a non-profit or as a private entity. Non-profits are more likely to advertise their dances in the Calendar of Events or entertainment sections of your local and weekly newspapers, which usually offer this space as a free service to these types of organizations. So check this area of your paper carefully.

Ballroom and country western (C/W) dances are usually privately run by studios and dance instructors, who tend to advertise in newspapers, the Yellow Pages, or any other media they feel will reach their intended audience.

Resource Guide. To help you on your way, check the back of this book for a guide to some of the internet sites and dance organizations around the country. As you become more involved in social dancing you will find many more dance venues nearby than you thought.

> Selecting a dance is somewhat like choosing a wine. Everyone's taste is different.

Selecting a dance is somewhat like choosing a wine. Everyone's taste is different. So it is with dance. To help you get started, here are some questions you may want to ask:

Is a beginning lesson offered at the dance?

This is crucial, especially if you haven't had lessons before. Know at least a couple of steps before you go out on the dance floor. This is true whether you are leading or following. If a beginner's lesson is not offered, this is a perfect time to ask where you might find instruction in this kind of dance.

What is the age range of the crowd?

Age is an important consideration for many individuals. For instance, most people between 30 and 40 years old aren't interested in attending a dance where everyone else is over 65. And vice versa.

Some dances cater to an older crowd, others to college students, and others cover the spectrum of age. A number of night clubs offer different time slots oriented toward various age groups. One such club promotes the earlier time slot for the 30-50 year olds, and the later slot for the younger generation who want to stay out later. Each organization is different—it pays to check so as to avoid unnecessary awkwardness.

What kind of music is played? If there is a mixture, what can I expect?

Some swing clubs, for instance, play exclusively Lindy or

West Coast Swing music. Others offer a more liberal selection that may include both. Ballroom dancing inherently includes a mixture of smooth-style and Latin-style music. Chapter 7 defines music and dance styles more clearly.

Is the music taped or live, or is there a deejay?

The answer tells you what you're getting for your money. Also inherent in the question is the preference of live over recorded music. A live band (as opposed, perhaps, to a dead one?) offers a certain ambiance not attainable with recorded music. The difference is akin to listening to recorded music at home and attending a concert. In the first instance, you are certain of the quality, and your ability to satisfy your desire is limited solely by your musical library. Attending a live concert provides an excitement and spontaneity unavailable with recorded music; the quality, as well as the range of the music is, however, subject to the limitations and versatility of the band. Many, if not most dance clubs will employ a deejay, so as to control costs and quality of the music.

Is there an admission charge? How much?

This way there are no unwelcome surprises.

Okay. Let's assume everything sounds good: there's the right kind of music and age mix, and a beginner's lesson is offered. Now decide whether to go alone or with a friend. My experience has shown a definite difference between the sexes. If you are a man, you will probably go alone, if for no other reason than it will be nearly impossible to get another male to go with you. It's the macho thing again. Later, after your social life takes off while your friends' are still on the ground, they may very well ask to come with you. At that point, congratulate them on their good sense and welcome them to your new-found passion.

If you are a woman, you will want female companionship on this journey. Women do seem to be more supportive of each other than men when it comes to this kind of thing, and I heartily recommend a companion if possible. There are, however, a few simple rules to follow when you are at the dance.

Make yourself visible. Do not find a table in the deepest, darkest corner of the room and sit there all night, watching and chatting away. Unless you are unusually attractive, this is a sure way to make certain you leave at the end of the evening without touching the dance floor—unless on the way to the restroom. Even if you are fortunate enough to be so attractive that men will come looking for you, chances are they will be either the "experts" I mentioned earlier or the most confident dancers. While you may be thinking, "Having a confident dancer ask me onto the dance floor wouldn't be so bad," I have found that beginners often find it intimidating to dance with an experienced dancer. The greater the disparity in skills, the more self-conscious the novice tends to be. Besides, most good dancers don't want to spend all evening dancing with a beginner, so chances are that dancing is not exactly what he has on his mind.

> Do not find a table in the deepest, darkest corner of the room and sit there all night, watching and chatting away. Unless you are unusually attractive, this is a sure way to make certain you leave at the end of the evening without touching the dance floor—unless on the way to the restroom.

Position yourself near the dance floor. Doing so increases the chances of someone noticing you and asking you to dance. If you are a man, you will want to position yourself likewise, except that you are most likely the one to ask someone to dance. I was fortunate enough to have a couple of women invite me onto the dance floor the first time I went to the club, and I'm sure they did so because they saw I was a newcomer. The vast majority of the time, however, I had to ask the women, at least until I became a more accomplished dancer and they sought my company.

Encourage men to ask you. If you are a woman, don't sit facing away from the dance floor and chatting with your girlfriend all evening. Men are less likely to approach two women deep in conversation who appear as if they have no desire to dance. No one likes to be rejected. The signal you're sending out, whether you realize it or not, is, "Stay away. We're not particularly interested in dancing with you right now." So if you are looking to dance, face the dance floor and smile encouragingly at those men who look your way.

Wear something to stimulate conversation. This is optional, of course, and may not get you a lot of extra dances, but it certainly will give your dance partner an additional subject to talk about on and off the dance floor.

My sister and I used to practice together, and occasionally when we went out with some other club members we wound up dancing together. No one outside our group ever asked either of us to dance. This was especially unusual for my sister, who is very attractive. We talked about it and finally decided it was because people thought we were a couple when we danced. To take care of that misunderstanding, we decided to order some T-shirts, one with "Brother" and the other with "Sister" written on them. My sister found a dance partner before we had a chance to use them, but I'm sure they would have made for some interesting conversation, as well as clearing up any misunderstanding on the part of others watching us.

I strongly suggest that you do not plan to "just observe" the first night (unless you are only scouting out the various dances, as I suggested earlier). As an observer you are likely to become intimidated. Everyone on the dance floor is going to look great to you. It will not take long before you have convinced yourself that:

a) You'll never be that good, so why bother trying, or

b) Nobody's going to want to dance with you.

I remember when I started out. I was sure that none of the women would want to dance with me. Every time I asked a woman to dance I felt as if I were asking her to do penance. Really! I had taken only the one basic lesson and knew all of two steps, and I just kept turning my partner first one way, then the other. All I could think of was how boring it must be for this poor woman who was stuck with me for those three minutes on the dance floor! Yet

> **in a social dance situation a dance is just a dance, nothing more. It is not a proposition of any kind other than "will you spend three minutes on the dance floor with me?"**

week after week I kept coming back, asking the same girls to dance, and I don't recall ever being turned down. Not once. Why? I can't say for sure.

It is certainly not because women by nature are too compassionate to say *no*. I mean, I've asked enough of them to dance in the past and have been rejected often enough to know that "no" is not a term females are unfamiliar with. I've come to the conclusion that there are two basic reasons that account for this generosity. First, and probably foremost, in a social dance situation a dance is just a dance, nothing more. It is not a proposition of any kind other than "will you spend three minutes on the dance floor with me?" It's not very easy to say "no" to something as innocuous as that. Women *do* seem to have extraordinary compassion for the poor guy who's put his male ego on the line in what has traditionally been a female-dominated sport. They fully recognize that the man has the more difficult role in the early stages, since he has to lead in addition to learning the footwork and other body motions. That compassion, however, soon turns to cool appraisal if they sense that anything more is at stake.

Another contributing factor to their generosity may be the idea that "Here is a potential dance partner. Let's not waste any opportunity."

If you're a female reading this, I'm going to tell you right now that ladies who are willing to ask for dances get the most dances. I tell this to all the women who come to our workshops before they go to our weekly dance. The typical response is, "I could never do that! I don't have the nerve!" Chapter 6 has tips on how to make this process more comfortable. For the moment, consider the following:

> **By asking, you accomplish two things. You take the initiative, thereby increasing the pool of men to choose from, instead of waiting for them to select you among a large number of women.**

Usually in the position of pursuer, men are not trained to say "no," as women are. Think about the male ego. How many men do you think have had a woman come up to them asking them to dance? Very few indeed. Moreover, we go right back to those three minutes on the dance floor. A dance is only a dance. I've never rejected a woman's request for a dance unless I physically couldn't dance or, didn't know how to do that particular kind of dance—valid reasons for not trotting right onto the dance floor. Otherwise, I'll always dance upon request, and so will 99 percent of all the other men at a dance. So there's nothing to be scared or nervous about. Really!

When you ask, you become less dependent on your looks or skill as a dancer. It is a fact of life that women outnumber men at most dances. Fortunately, it is also customary and therefore perfectly acceptable in this type of setting for a woman to ask a man for a dance.

By asking, you accomplish two things. You take the initiative, thereby increasing the pool of men to choose from, instead of waiting for them to select you among a large number of women. Taking the initiative provides you with more opportunities to meet men and build relationships. In addition, you wind up dancing more, thereby having more fun while you become a better dancer. It is very difficult to get better watching from the sidelines.

No matter what teachers of dancing may assert, the most expedient and certainly the best way to learn to dance is to stand up and try it; no one can ever learn by sitting quietly and looking on.

—George E. Wilson,
Wilson's Ball-Room Guide and Call Book

Taking the initiative provides you with more opportunities to meet men and build relationships. In addition, you wind up dancing more, thereby having more fun while you become a better dancer. It is very difficult to get better watching from the sidelines.

When I was just beginning, a few of the female dancers asked me onto the dance floor. As I became a better dancer, I tried to return the favor by asking some of the women who had been sitting at the side for a while. Not all men do this, however. Even if they did, there isn't anyone keeping score to see who danced how often. Ask, and ye shall receive.

As for the idea that you will never be as good as the other dancers, I can assure you that not everyone on the dance floor is as good as you may think. They may look like they know what they're doing, and they probably do know more than you, but not much more. Sure, there are going to be a few really good dancers out there, but you are not competing with them. In fact, you are not competing with anyone, except perhaps yourself and your own fears. You will be surprised, if you stick with it, how fast you will catch up to many of those dancers who now look so good to you. As you improve, you will probably find that some of the people you had thought were really talented are not as exceptional as you first thought. In fact, you might change your mind about who some of the better dancers are. Eventually, with a little practice, you may become one of them.

If, by some chance, you find your requests for a dance being continually rejected, it means either that you have a personal hygiene problem or you've stumbled across something more akin to the singles scene than a social dance group. It can happen.

I mentioned earlier that the type of dance usually determines the crowd. Although this is true, there are other contributing factors, such as the people or organization running the event, the demographics of the dancers, and so on. Plenty of dance clubs cater to different age groups and different style dances. Look around until you find one you feel comfortable with. It may take a little effort, but it will be well worth it.

To summarize the advice on how to get started:

1. Select the type of dance you want to learn. Consider:
music
opportunity/frequency
proximity
atmosphere

2. Locate potential dance clubs or other organizations by checking:

the *Resource Guide* in this book

the Calendar of Events and entertainment sections of your newspaper

the Yellow Pages under: Dance studios; Dancing instruction; Night clubs; Clubs; Dance clubs; Adult education programs; YMCA; Community center; Local recreation council; Community college

3. Visit potential dance sites. Talk to other dancers. Ask questions to make sure that a dance group/class/session fulfills your needs for:

beginner's dance lessons

age range

type of music

admission charge

4. When you go:

Make yourself visible.

Situate yourself near the dance floor.

Encourage people to ask you.

Ask for a dance.

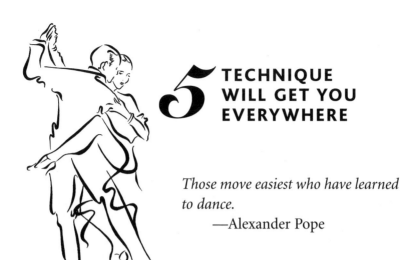

5 TECHNIQUE WILL GET YOU EVERYWHERE

Those move easiest who have learned to dance.
—Alexander Pope

Knowledge is power. Everything else being equal, the more knowledgeable we are at our job, the more invaluable we become to our employer. It is much the same in sports. Substitute the word technique for knowledge—technique is, after all, acquired knowledge manifested physically—and the appropriateness of the analogy becomes immediately obvious. The skier or golfer who has invested the time to acquire the proper technique is more likely to excel than the individual who flies by the seat of his pants. So it is with dance—except even more so—since we dance as partners. In fact, dancing today is probably more of an equal partnership than ever before.

When my parents danced, and they were relatively good Lindy dancers, my mother did most of the footwork. My father, for the most part, led or "threw" my mother out and let her do her thing—which she did quite well. Today, both men and women are expected to be active participants; that is to say that each one should add something to the dance. This is where knowledge (technique) comes into play. The more knowledge you possess, the more interesting you become as a partner. As nationally renowned dance instructor Skippy Blair puts it, "The first dance with someone is the same as a first conversation. If it is a 'one-sided' conversation, it is very dull."

> **Perhaps the single most important fundamental element that the man must learn is how to lead properly.**

Equal partnership stresses the need for women to take dance lessons as well as men. The more your technique improves, the more actively you can follow and the more exciting—and desirable—you will become as a dance partner.

Perhaps the single most important fundamental element that the man must learn is how to lead properly. Simply put, this means he must be able to clearly indicate to his partner what his intentions are. This is not as simple in practice as one would think. I have spoken to a number of women who were disappointed after dancing with an acknowledged competition dance champion. They couldn't seem to "connect" and felt it was their fault. It turned out to be the opposite. When I asked them questions about his lead, it became obvious he was not communicating his intentions well. He was, in fact, a poor leader—not an unheard of trait among competition dancers. Competition dancers are used to dancing with a single partner in a choreographed manner. Unless they dance socially with different partners, there is little need for them to learn how to lead well. All of which shows that no matter how good a dancer you are, you must be able to communicate with your partner if you want her to feel that special tingle in her spine when the two of you connect on the dance floor.

Dance lessons also help you understand the fundamentals of either moving a partner or being directed by your partner around the dance floor. Once you know how to do that well, the only thing that differs is the type of dance that accompanies a particular type of music. The basics do not change. In other words, once you learn how to perform one dance well, learning other dances becomes easier. The Lindy, West Coast Swing, the Bop, and the various forms of Shag all use the same technique for partnering, the same rhythm, and the same or similar types of turns. There is a basic skeleton to all these dances so you can go from one dance to another relatively easily. But you must first build your foundation of knowledge.

While there is no particular order to learning social dancing, there are certain dances that are considered *foundational* dances; that is to say that these dances have many steps that are common to other dances of their type, yet they are relatively easy to learn. For instance, the fox trot—a smooth-style ballroom dance—is a foundational dance. The fox trot *box step* is the same as the waltz *box step* and the rumba *box step*. There are differences in tempos and foot placement, but the basic step is identical.

The fox trot and rumba are both foundational ballroom dances. Jeff Allen, in his excellent book, *Quickstart to Social Dancing*, teaches the fox trot, waltz, rumba, merengue, swing, and cha-cha in precisely that order so as to maximize the incorporation of step patterns and concepts learned from one dance to another.

West Coast Swing, on the other hand, is a relatively difficult dance to learn, and it might be advisable to first take a few lessons in one of the other swing dances. This is not absolutely necessary, of course, but you will have an easier time of it if you are already familiar with basic six- and eight-count rhythm when you enter a WCS class.

Skippy Blair, sometimes affectionately known as the "teacher's teacher," has attached levels to each of the dances, including West Coast Swing and Lindy. (These can be found in Chapter 7.) She suggests that ballroom dancing students begin with nightclub slow dance (rhythm fox trot), basic salsa, and basic rumba. By starting with these three dances, you will learn to dance to three different kinds of music, each with a different "feeling," while using three different sets of foot positions. In learning these dances, you will obtain the rhythm, feeling and movement that will allow you to dance to almost any piece of music.

You can save yourself a lot of money—not to mention frustration—by being an educated consumer.

Skippy's system is not carved in stone, and many dance instructors would probably disagree with levels ascribed to certain dances. There is no question, however, that her methods are being used successfully by many dance instructors around the country. Use her system—or at least refer to it—and you will have more control over your dancing destiny. You can save yourself a lot of money—not to mention frustration—by being an educated consumer.

(Note: Nightclub slow dance, otherwise known as rhythm fox trot, does not progress around a line of dance. It tends to be danced in a small area of the dance floor, as are West Coast and East Coast Swing, rumba and many of the Latin dances.)

Now let's take a look at the four types of lessons: group, private, workshops, and videotapes.

GROUP LESSONS

The primary advantage of group lessons is that you get to meet other people in a social dance setting. Since the primary purpose of learning how to partner dance is to improve our social life, it is best experienced in a social setting—that is to say, with other people. You will learn dance steps and patterns, as well as the principles of movement and partnering. You will learn all of this while satisfying the great social aspect of social dance.

Classes offer the opportunity to dance with different partners, which enables you to become a better leader and follower. Some women respond to a lighter touch. Others need more direction. Some men provide a stronger lead than others. The weaker leads force a woman to become more aware as a follower. The end result is that you will become a better dancer.

The primary advantage of group lessons is that you get to meet other people in a social dance setting.

The dance instructor is usually a good source of information about local dances where you can practice what he or she is teaching you. You may want to talk to some of the participants in the group and see if they are interested in joining together and going to one of these dances. Since you all know the same patterns, it will alleviate some of the awkwardness of the first night on the dance floor. This is a perfect opportunity to find a practice partner. You don't have to be romantically attracted to him or her. All you are looking for is someone to practice with after class.

Group lessons are fairly inexpensive compared to private. They are usually offered in a series, as few as four and as many as eight one-hour sessions. Prices vary depending on the type of dance, the city where you live, and the prominence of the studio or instructor. Anything in the range of $5 to $15 per lesson can be considered within the norm. On the other hand, for individual lessons you can expect to pay $50 and up for a one-hour session. Most dance studio chains sell units that include one private lesson, one practice session, and one class. These units often cost $85 or more.

If you decide to take group lessons there is always the

Catch-22 of steps versus technique. Beginning students tend to be primarily interested in learning steps, not realizing it is the technique that allows you to do the movement. Technique, however, is a subtle thing and not learned quickly so it's up to the dance instructor to strike a balance between the two so the student does not get bored. You'll find this balance differs with each instructor.

Men, who have so much to learn in the beginning concerning footwork and arm leads, may want to consider private lessons so they can appear less awkward in front of women.

No two instructors are quite the same in the way they teach. Both methods and emphasis differ. So if you're not satisfied with the instructor you start with, search for another until you find one with whom you feel comfortable.

The world cares very little about what a man or woman knows; it is what a man or woman is able to do that counts.
—Booker T. Washington

PRIVATE LESSONS

Private lessons, to some extent, are the antithesis of the concept of social dancing. By their very nature, they are isolating; therefore they do not satisfy the social aspect of partner dancing. Yet they serve an important function in the learning process, and can be extremely helpful in certain situations.

Some people, for example, are extremely awkward or shy and benefit from private lessons to help them get past the initial learning phase. If you find dancing a struggle, or feel yourself getting frustrated, a couple of private lessons may be of tremendous value. Men, who have so much to learn in the beginning concerning footwork and arm leads, may want to consider private lessons so they can appear less awkward in front of women. You will save yourself a great deal of frustration in the long run because you get comfortable sooner and learn faster.

Private lessons allow you to proceed at your own pace. Whereas in a group lesson the instructor has to proceed at a pace that is comfortable for the class, with individual instruction you can move along as fast as your talent and dedication allow.

Private lessons, on the other hand, are more expensive than group lessons and you do not experience the benefit of meeting and dancing with other people, so the social aspect that can be gained from group lessons is lost. It is also possible you can be fooled into thinking you are better than you really are because you have no one for comparison.

I've encountered this myself. I was taking some fox trot lessons and found myself leading the instructor around the room quite well. However, when I attempted the same moves with non-professional partners, they failed to respond as I had expected. The problem is that good instructors are so "tuned in" that they can follow almost any lead, no matter how weak. Also, female pros tend to "back lead" their students to help them. Some instructors try to offset this tendency by trying to make it difficult, but it is not the same as dancing with one's peers. I eventually decided to deal with this problem by bringing someone I felt comfortable with (in other words, someone I didn't mind feeling foolish in front of) to my lesson, and letting the instructor teach both of us. This provided me with two advantages. I had to learn to lead someone who didn't already know how to dance the fox trot, and I had someone to practice with after the lesson.

Many dance instructors recommend that you take a combination of private and group lessons for maximum benefit. You can use private lessons in conjunction with group classes to speed up the learning process, or you can arrange for a private lesson when you feel you are having trouble getting past a certain point in the class. You can also use it to fix a problem in your dancing. Afterward, continue with the group classes until you feel the need for another private lesson.

"Technique allows us to go beyond the steps, hear something in the music, feel the connection, and share the goose bumps."

Fred Astaire Studios employ a more organized, but similar system in teaching their students. According to dance instructor Andy McCann, the 3 Way System suggests taking the class lesson before a private one. The reason, according to Andy, is that "all of the patterns are the same for everyone, but individual ability and needs differ. Therefore, the instructor makes careful note of the classes (and level) attended by his/her particular student and then, during the private lessons gears the instruction to add the needed technique and style to those patterns. (Under the 3 way system, patterns are not taught in private lessons, only in classes.) When the instructor feels the student has grasped the content, he or she is told to attend a practice session or party to practically apply those patterns and learned techniques under social conditions with various partners."

I have found private lessons to be of great help in fine-tuning my technique. This is difficult to do in a group environment. Students in a class usually want to learn steps. Many get bored when the instructor concentrates on technique. Yet it is the technique that will make others want to dance with you. As Skippy Blair says, "Technique allows us to go beyond the steps, hear something in the music, feel the connection, and share the goose bumps."

It is difficult to convince a beginner—and sometimes

even experienced dancers—that it is better to be able to perform a few basic steps with grace and style than blunder through a complicated routine. If you are interested in learning good technique so as to become a desired dance partner, it is a good idea to invest in some private lessons.

> **Dancing is a team sport, and nothing can happen without good communication.**

My own experience offers a good example. I started with a beginner lesson and then learned steps from some of the better dancers at the club. This was fine up to a point, but I found something missing from my dancing. I had the footwork down, but for some reason my dance partners didn't seem to know what I wanted them to do. I also never felt as smooth as I wanted. Then I met Margaret Batiuchok, a professional dance champion and instructor from New York City, who gave an exhibition at one of our dances. I found her style of swing, sometimes referred to as a smooth Savoy-style Lindy, very appealing, and I decided to take a private lesson with her. My intentions were merely to learn a few new moves for the dance floor.

At our first session she danced with me for about 30 seconds and then proceeded to show me the proper way to hold her hand! My first thoughts were: this wasn't what I had paid for; I just wanted to learn some new steps similar to the ones she had demonstrated. I kept my disappointment to myself, however, and with the picture of her moving so gracefully around the dance floor still fresh in my mind, I decided to remain quiet and give her a chance.

Margaret taught me at least one new step or pattern in each lesson, but she emphasized technique. Each time we met, we would review previous step patterns, with Margaret correcting any flaws that she detected in my movement. She was even more insistent with regard to my communicating my intentions to my partner. Dancing is a team sport, and nothing can happen without good communication. In dancing, this is known as the art of leading. As you can imagine, this process does not occur overnight. In today's society, we want things to happen quickly, without effort. Lose weight without eating less. Develop great abs in less than five minutes per day. Learn to speak Italian by osmosis. For most people, effort is required to become better at whatever it is they want to become better at. So it goes with dance. Still, it was not long before I noticed a change beginning to take place. More and more, my partners complimented me on my ability to lead. Within a few months, my improved technique had taken my social dancing to a new level. I've taken lessons from other instructors in styles that I find equally interesting, but I will always owe Margaret a debt of gratitude for instilling in me those dance fundamentals that have helped me learn any new dance step.

If their feet aren't in the right place, at least their hearts are.
—Christian M. Chensvold,
on novice swingers

WORKSHOPS

Workshops are a special category of classes or group lessons. Typically, a special instructor with a unique style is brought in to teach a class. Such classes may last a period of hours or may include a weekend. In some instances, there is a series of workshops. It's important to understand what you can expect to get out of such sessions. Having organized quite a few of these, I have come to the conclusion that most dancers and would-be dancers attend workshops with unrealistic expectations.

Workshops, by their very nature, are step-oriented. Rather than teaching technique, the instructor emphasizes dance patterns. This occurs for several reasons. Foremost is that the instructor wants to get the class excited about his or her style of dance. This is not going to happen if he or she concentrates on technique.

People attend workshops to learn patterns. The vast majority of students are not satisfied with learning only one or two new steps. They want five or ten. Forget the fact that they couldn't possibly learn that many in a week, much less a day. That's what they want. So the instructor is under pressure to give this to them.

So is there any point to attending a workshop? The answer is yes, if you understand why you are taking it and what is reasonable to expect from it.

There also tends to be quite a mixed level of dance experience in these workshops, even though participants are usually separated into skill categories. Dancers, like all people, have their own opinions of how advanced they are, and the way they see themselves is often not the way others see them. A dance instructor teaching a weekly class can more easily move people into the appropriate skill level. This is not as simple in a one-day class.

So is there any point to attending a workshop? The answer is yes, if you understand why you are taking it and what is reasonable to expect from it.

Workshops are an opportunity to get introduced to a new style of dance. See if you like it. If you do, then find out if the instructor lives close enough so you can follow up with some lessons, or if there is someone in your area who teaches that style. Perhaps the workshop instructor offers a videotape that will allow you the benefit of continued practice to really learn the sequences well, and you may even be able to pick up some techniques from the video.

Plan on taking one, or at most two patterns of the five or

ten shown to you, and incorporating them into your dance repertoire. Then make sure you practice those moves as soon as possible so as to instill them into your memory. Follow that up by trying them out with different dance partners at your next dance. If you do that, you should have them available as part of your regular dance routine within two to three weeks.

Workshops are a great way to meet new people who have a similar interest—dance. Some attend because they want to try a different dance. Others have never danced before, but see the workshop advertised and figure they will give it a try, realizing that dance is a great way to meet people in a friendly environment. In other words, they are like you; they are looking for a dance partner, a practice partner, or perhaps a life partner.

By the way, if the style of dance that's advertised really stimulates your interest, look around for other workshops the same instructor is offering. You may have to travel a bit, but many members of our club have done so and found the fun to be worth the travel. Some have wound up dating people they met at a workshop. Expand your horizons.

Whatever women do they must do twice as well as men to be thought half as good. Luckily, this is not difficult.
—Charlotte Whitton

VIDEOTAPES

Many sources of instructional videotapes are available for almost any type of social dance. I list a few of these sources in the *Resource Guide*. Most dance instructors agree that while videotapes have their place, they are not a substitute for dance lessons.

Professional dance instructor Paul Grecki points out that videotapes won't teach you how to dance. You won't be able to pick up the "feel" of the dance. For that, you need an instructor who can take you in his or her arms and help you get that feeling. Learning a new move is a matter of muscle memory. You need to feel it and do it. Only then will you remember it.

Paul does feel that videotapes can benefit dancers who have gotten past the awkwardness of the early learning experience and have a little understanding of the dance they are doing. At this point you can learn some material quickly because tapes are usually step-oriented and you can review them over and over. However, if you have a question, you can't ask the tape, so you will probably require an instructor to fine-tune your moves.

Sherry Palencia, a country western dance instructor, shares many of Paul's concerns. Only after some experience "can you discriminate whether a videotape is worthwhile," she says. Paul agrees. Some videotapes are so precise in breaking down the moves, "even I get bored, and I do this for a living."

The most obvious disadvantage to the exclusive use of videotapes as a learning tool is the lack of social interaction. You are learning how to dance because of its social aspect. You want to meet new people—as many as possible, especially POS. On the other hand, inviting a group of people from the dance club to your home for a dance video party may be a novel way of expanding your circle of friends with the same interest you have. Alternatively, a quiet evening at home may provide the breather you need with all the new excitement in your life.

HOW TO CHOOSE A STUDIO

Okay, let's say you've decided you want to take lessons but aren't sure how to go about choosing a dance studio. Here are some tips from Larry Schulz, co-owner and business manager of the Sandra Cameron Dance Center in New York City.

1. Determine what you want to study. Social dancing and competition dancing are very different, and it's rare—albeit not impossible—that a studio can do both well. Social dance is about learning to express yourself. You are taught a common vocabulary of steps, as well as a basic technique of movement and partnering. Hopefully, you will then take that and bring your own individuality to it and create something unique.

Competition dancing, on the other hand, is not about personal expression; it is about perfecting the technique. If you watch an international style ballroom dance competition, everyone will appear to look similar in terms of the steps and the technique, which is set down and codified and established by the Imperial Society of Teachers of Dancing. The differences lie in their execution, not their expression.

The emphasis on personal expression in social dance on the one hand, and the emphasis on technique in competition dancing on the other, makes it difficult for a studio or instructor to accommodate both. You may therefore want to ask the studio which type of dance they teach—social or competition.

2. Consider whether you want to take private or group lessons. We encourage students to study in groups, at least initially. In this way you're introduced to the whole experience of dancing with other people, and that's what social dancing is all about. If you study privately, you learn a skill with one person, and on some level you get the idea that you can perform that skill with only one person.

3. When you walk into a studio, find out how much classes cost. Ask for a brochure or flyer with all the costs.

Everything should be very up front. There should be no mystery as to how much this experience is going to cost.

4. You should feel comfortable in the studio. If you feel pressured, steered into studying privately, or pushed into taking other kinds of classes, that's not right.

5. Ask around for information or opinions. Ask about the studio, the kind of instructors, and the level of the instructors. Are the teachers qualified? Are the teachers good dancers?

If you are at a dance and see someone dancing well, go up to him or her and say, "I really like your style of dancing. Where did you learn?" Anyone who dances really well has studied it, because there's a technique and knowledge base of information that has to be learned.

> A teacher can only teach what he or she knows. In terms of basic steps, almost anybody can teach them. But the better the teacher, the better the information and the better you're going to learn it.

6. Go to a social or practice session. Dance studios usually have a Friday or Saturday night social where students can practice with the instructors present. Watch how the people dance. Watch how the staff dances. If the dancing doesn't look very good—if it looks weird, forced, or arched—that's what you are going to be taught. A teacher can only teach what he or she knows. In terms of basic steps, almost anybody can teach them. But the better the teacher, the better the information and the better you're going to learn it.

CONTRACTS

One of the most controversial issues among dance instructors and dance studios is the use of contracts. Many independent studios and dance instructors avoid the use of contracts entirely.

Proponents of contracts will argue that it provides you with a written agreement stating what you are supposed to receive for your money. This agreement will define what type of lessons are available, how long the lessons are, how payments are made, what constitutes a request for a refund of the unused portion, and other important issues. Without a contract you have nothing to indicate what you are supposed to receive for your investment.

Secondly, written agreements require you to study dancing in a more logical format. A course of instruction is chosen after determining your personal objective. This includes the things that your instructor believes you need to study over the next few weeks or months in order to achieve a high degree of success in obtaining your goals. An independent studio with no formal course of instruction—and a contract specifying the details of that instruction—offers immense freedom, but provides no set objective and little or no organization. This is like studying economics at a local community college and dropping in for a class whenever you feel like it.

National chain studios such as Arthur Murray International and Fred Astaire use "enrollment agreements," not contracts. According to Arthur Murray International, enrollment agreements can be cancelled at any time for any reason. Any unused portion of the enrollment agreement must be refunded less a small service fee that is set by agreement with the Federal Trade Commission (FTC).

In order to be state compliant, the specifics in enrollment agreements vary from state to state. Enrollment agreements within the state, however, should be similar, although not necessarily exactly the same. Different provisions may be included depending on the agreement between student, instructor, and studio operator. Also, since each studio is independently owned, some studios may offer different features. For instance, some studios may allow a student more flexibility in attending group dance classes with no additional charge, while other studios may be much more rigid.

(Note: Independent studios do not come under the FTC regulations and therefore can utilize contracts which are *binding*.)

Opponents of contracts, which include many of the independent studios and instructors, will argue that if the school is really interested in teaching you, their job is to teach you well. And if they teach you well, you will, of your own volition, keep coming back. On the other hand, if you are not happy with your instructor or the school, you will stop attending classes. The matter of a refund becomes moot, since there is no contract or enrollment agreement to begin with.

Some independent studios and many private instructors will allow you to commit to either a series of classes or a certain number of hours. This latter option is especially advantageous to the engaged couple who need to learn a few basic steps in order to dance at their wedding reception.

Regarding the course of instruction, you would be well advised to judge the independent studio according to what is happening at that studio. Review the syllabus. Does the studio offer courses that will take you from a basic or beginner's level to intermediate and advanced levels for the different dances that they teach? If it offers these on a regular basis, and the studio meets the criteria discussed earlier, the chances are that it can help you achieve your goals.

CHAIN OR INDEPENDENT STUDIO?

The national chain studios offer both social and competition dancing. Approximately ten percent of Arthur Murray students compete in tournaments. A student will begin at the

Bronze level and, with enough lessons and practice, gradually work his or her way up to the Silver and finally, Gold level. Each advance in level is achieved through competitions sponsored by the national chain. This provides an inherent, built-in system of motivation for the student to continue, using a tangible goal along with a clear path to achieving that goal. The course requires continual private lessons, which form the basis of the syllabus or curriculum.

> **"What do you want to study— social dancing or competition dancing?"**

The advantage to this type of competitive dancing is that it sets a standard to work toward. The disadvantage is that, since everyone is being judged on the same style, the focus is not on learning how to express oneself on an individual basis. Rather, the focus is on technique. So we go back to the question, "What do you want to study—social dancing or competition dancing?"

Independent studios are just that—independent. Therefore, each will have its own emphasis and syllabus. Since you are ostensibly reading this book to achieve a better social life through social dancing, it is only a matter of common sense that you orient your study of dance in such a way as to increase your social contact. That being the case, you will want to look for a studio that emphasizes social dance. These types of studios often have a syllabus that is heavily tilted toward group classes, with private lessons available for all of the reasons we have already discussed.

While I personally have chosen to study with independent instructors and studios, I know numerous dancers who have taken lessons with chain studios such as Arthur Murray International and swear by it. These dance students often attend dances and other dance-related events together, with the result being a terrific social life. They also have numerous opportunities to participate in dance contests. So, it really is a matter of personal preference and how much money you are willing to spend.

Studios are not the only place to learn how to dance, of course. Some types of dance—contra dancing, for example—won't even be found in most studios. Country western lessons are available in many places these days, from bars to service club halls such as the Elks, American Legions, and Knights of Columbus. Ballroom dancing, on the other hand, is taught mainly in studios and community education classes by private instructors. A quick look in the back of this book will give you an idea as to where you may want to start checking for lessons in your area.

PARTNERING

One of the often-asked questions from beginners is, "Am I better off dancing with numerous partners or just one?" Although there is no carved-in-stone response to this question, most instructors feel that the advantage goes to having numerous partners. Besides the obvious advantage for a single person who wants to meet as many people as possible, dancing with a variety of people gives you a greater variety of responses. In the end, experience will make you a better leader or follower.

Paul Grecki points out too that beginners have a tendency to blame others for their mistakes. The problem is that neither partner is competent enough to figure out who is to blame. By changing partners, you gain the following advantages:

1. You learn faster. You can't cover for each other, as do some couples who dance together all the time. People who dance together can develop bad habits. The guy may begin to cover for a gal's lack of follow, or the gal covers for her partner's lack of lead. I wince every time a woman tells me as we are walking onto the dance floor that she is a strong follower. *Translation: She wants to lead.*

2. Either it works or it doesn't. No faking it here. If you are the man, you may be able to dismiss one or two partners not following your lead. But if most, or none of the ladies are following you, take a close look at your technique. Same with the ladies. If you feel off balance, it may be your partner's fault for putting you into awkward positions. On the other hand, if you are always off balance in the turns and spins, you are doing something wrong.

Remember, you are partners for only a short time. If you don't get along, don't worry. It's only three minutes.

As you improve, you may want to get a dance partner. In this way you will have someone who knows the same moves you do and can dance at the same level. It's like playing tennis. If the person on the other side of the net can't hit the ball back, you are going to get frustrated. There are times you want to be able to use your best moves, to dance "full-out." For this, you need someone who is familiar with your style. This person doesn't have to be a romantic partner. As I mentioned earlier, for a while I practiced with my sister. We had a great time dancing together on occasion, but I can assure you that the majority of our time on the dance floor was spent with others. We knew, however, that when we did dance together, we could do all our moves.

No move is too tricky, no spin too excessive. For my partner.
—John Hayes

PRACTICE

Practice is an integral part of learning how to dance. You can't expect to improve if you walk into dance class without having spent some time during the week dancing, any more than you would expect to learn if you attended an academic course without studying between classes. It is simply a matter of memory reinforcement, nothing more.

Fortunately, dance practice is not like the homework assignments we were given in school. Dancing is fun and inherently social, not to mention great exercise. We've discussed in detail the fun and social aspects of dancing. What many people don't realize is that if you were to dance regularly you would build stamina equal to that of soccer players or runners. The physical stamina is far more lasting than that acquired by football or baseball players, who "stop and start" rather than move continuously. So you may want to consider your practice sessions a form of aerobic exercise. Lest I forget, this physical conditioning comes without the risk of injury inherent in most physical sports.

In order to dance well, your body has to become familiar with the step pattern so it can perform the move immediately when called upon. The time required for this to occur varies from person to person, depending on past experience and talent. Men, in general, experience a longer learning curve than women. Practicing only 15 minutes per day, however, combined with one dance evening per week, should be enough to provide a solid foundation for the move. Utilizing this method I found that within three weeks I had the move "down" to where I could perform it at will.

This practice scenario tends to fall into line with the "rules" often espoused in books dedicated to learning mental and verbal skills. Such books often advise daily practice of short duration the first week; less frequently thereafter. After three weeks, the skill becomes ingrained and remains as long as you continue to use it. A similar system for muscle memory makes sense. More is not necessarily better, however. Our attention span is finite, and longer practice periods may result in diminishing returns.

HOW TO PRACTICE

1. First you will need some space—approximately 5 ft. by 8 ft. should be sufficient. Hardwood floors are preferable since they will give you a smooth, flexible surface. Cement floors are hard on the joints—especially the back—so you may want to wear sneakers to help absorb the shock. If you decide to practice in your driveway or garage as I've done on occasion, feel free to invite the neighbors.

> **Music should match your taste and ability; neither too fast nor too slow.**

2. Select appropriate music. Music should match your taste and ability; neither too fast nor too slow. You should be able to move your feet comfortably in time to the music. If you can move your feet to the rhythm without losing the rhythm, you have the right music. If you cannot, it's probably too fast. Use music with correct tempos for the dance you are practicing. Refer to the *Resource Guide* for assistance, if necessary.

3. You may prefer to use a CD player since it will have a repeat function, making it easier to replay a particular song. CD players also provide clear prompts so you can easily locate the music you wish to play.

4. Try to get a feel for the rhythm of the music. Forget the melody and listen to the drum or rhythm line. The drum provides the beat. Once you have a sense of the rhythm, the steps will fit in more easily.

5. Don't become frustrated. Remember, short, frequent practice sessions are better than long, infrequent ones.

Practice time does not always have to be "set aside," however. For any dance, there are basic foot patterns that one must get comfortable with before progress is possible. In swing dance, something known as the triple step—a slight

variation of the basic single step—is usually taught to beginners. Because the move can be practiced "in place," I found
myself doing this while standing in line at the supermarket
or anywhere else that offered an idle moment. A few people
may have wondered what I was doing, but most probably
didn't even notice. Of course, I live in New York, so it would
take something extraordinary to get someone's attention.

Dance lessons and practice will improve your technique,
and good technique, like flattery, will get you everywhere. In
the meantime, find the music you enjoy and can dance comfortably to, and have fun. The rest will come with time.

Dancing is like bank robbery. It takes split-second timing.
—Twyla Tharp, in *Ms.* (1976)

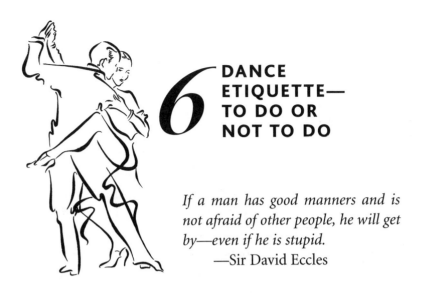

6 DANCE ETIQUETTE— TO DO OR NOT TO DO

If a man has good manners and is not afraid of other people, he will get by—even if he is stupid.
—Sir David Eccles

L et's say you've found a dance venue that suits you. It has all the right ingredients: good music, friendly people (at least the bartender greeted you as you entered), and the right age group; your parents aren't here, and neither are your children. You might have come by yourself, or you brought a friend. Even better, you arrived with some people from your dance class. And just for good measure, you've avoided that safe-looking corner table in the back of the room and instead opted for the one closest to the dance floor. In other words, you're ready. Slightly nervous, but ready. What's next?

If this is a dance club, consider introducing yourself to the people running the show. They should be more than happy to help you get started on the dance floor. In addition, they can provide you with valuable information about the club, such as past and future events.

Ballroom dance studios should have information available on weekly and monthly activities offered outside of classes. Ballroom dance events are usually similar to those offered by dance clubs, and therefore can be approached in much the same way.

The club leader may introduce you to some of the other

dancers. In our dance club, for instance, we have a group of board members who help new people, either by getting them involved in the beginner's lesson or—if the newcomers already have some dance experience—by enticing them onto the dance floor. We often make use of our more experienced dancers for this kind of help, so don't be surprised if you find yourself kicking up your heels with one of the people you were just admiring on the dance floor. Try not to be overly intimidated by an experienced dancer.

If dancers are really good they won't embarrass you by trying to make you do steps beyond your capability.

So often I hear from new members that they don't want to dance with someone because he or she is so good! Nonsense! If dancers are really good they won't embarrass you by trying to make you do steps beyond your capability. And they may also offer some worthwhile tips to improve your dancing. Remember, these people didn't just hop on the dance floor and perform the steps they do now. They were beginners once too! They took lessons somewhere along the way. These are the best people to learn from, and as long as you don't overstay your welcome, they usually are among the most tolerant because they've been where you are right now. At the beginning. We all started there.

That said, there are some commonsense things you can do to avoid having even the most tolerant people turn their heads and walk away at the sight of you approaching. One sure method of becoming *persona non grata* is to ask the same person to dance over and over. Social dancers are usually more than happy to help a newcomer along by dancing with him or her once or twice in an evening. To expect more is expecting too much. Everyone is usually encouraged to rotate dance partners at these events anyway, so even if you weren't a beginner, the two of you probably wouldn't be dancing more than a couple of dances in a row. Your best bet is to assume that one or two dances per evening with an experienced dancer is all you can expect without fear of overstaying your welcome. After your dance is over, thank your partner and move on. If you're a gal and the guy wants to dance with you some more, he'll come to you. If you're a guy and you want to continue dancing with the gal—the chemistry seems right or whatever—your male inclination may be to press for another dance. My suggestion is to stifle the urge.

Remember the story I told you earlier about female club members preferring to dance with a good dancer rather than with Tom Cruise? This might be a good thing for men to keep in mind. Even if you think you look like Tom Cruise, the odds are that she wants to move on. If you really think something is there, wait until you see her on the side taking a breather. Then go up and try to talk to her. Just don't be surprised if someone whisks her away in the middle of your conversation. Trying to carry on a dialogue with someone at one of these dances can be like trying to have a conversation with someone while riding the chairlift to the top of a ski slope. Just as things get interesting, you hear her friends shouting from below, impatiently waiting for her to join them. Fortunately, there is always *après-ski*. Although there may not be a fireplace around which to continue your conversation at the end of the dance, there's usually a nearby diner or coffee shop. And you have just discovered a common interest in dancing to explore and develop.

You survived your first dance, left the floor by escorting—or being escorted by—your partner, thanked her or him, and went your separate ways. What now? If you're a guy, you have only one choice if you want to do some more dancing: you've got to ask. Fortunately for men, we're used to this. And once you find that rejection is a rare occurrence, it becomes easier. Most women, on the other hand, are not used to asking for a dance.

> **You don't want to be confined to dancing with only those people who ask you. In the long run you will have a better time and become a more accomplished dancer if you are willing to ask men. Not only is it acceptable behavior, it is customary.**

At one of our workshops I suggested the students try and attend our Tuesday dances since these would offer the best opportunity to practice. One woman, Anna, asked me what these dances were like, and I explained they were very friendly, and that it was perfectly acceptable for the women to ask the men to dance. She replied she could never do that. It just wasn't the way she had been brought up. I told her I understood, but it had been my experience that those women who were willing to ask got to dance more. You don't want to be confined to dancing with only those people who ask you. In the long run you will have a better time and become a more accomplished dancer if you are willing to ask men. Not only is it acceptable behavior, it is customary.

There is always a best way of doing everything, if it be to boil an egg. Manners are the happy ways of doing things; each once a stroke of genius or love,—now repeated and hardened into usage.

—Ralph Waldo Emerson,
The Conduct of Life

You may also spot someone performing a dance step that you want to learn. One time I and several members of our dance club were at Irving Plaza, a dance club in New York. There must have been at least three hundred people on the dance floor, and my friend Lisa spotted someone doing a dance step that she really liked. We tried, unsuccessfully, to figure out how the man performed the move. Lisa finally declared that she would just go over and ask him. And the guy, with his female partner watching, showed her! Now some might consider that being overly aggressive, but that was Lisa just being Lisa. The point is that she wasn't afraid to ask. (Several women have remarked that correct dance etiquette would have been for Lisa to ask the woman for permission first before approaching her partner. In retrospect I would agree with this.)

Anna did decide to attend our Tuesday dance the following week. Knowing how she felt about asking men to dance, I was afraid she might be disappointed, so in the middle of the evening I went over to her and asked how things were going. She was thrilled. She told me she had watched the people on the dance floor for a while, then gone up to one of the more skilled male dancers and asked, "How can a girl get a dance with a good dancer?" The male ego responded, as you might anticipate, and lo and behold, Anna found herself dancing with the best dancers in the place. The *way* in which she asked was not nearly as crucial as the fact that *she did ask.*

I've spoken with numerous female members and learned that in the beginning each had her own way of asking. A simple "Would you like to dance?" is sufficient. I suggest that you avoid the somewhat negative approach: "Would you mind dancing with me? I'm just beginning." Be as positive as you can. If the man is that concerned about your level of ability, he will ask you. Then you can cross him off *your* list. Leaders should dance at a level appropriate to the follower, and not show off. As you get to know everyone better, the verbal request usually shortens to some version of "Let's dance."

Remember, a dance is just a dance. This isn't the bar

scene where the dance is an acknowledged form of introduction, and where if you say "yes" you may be indicating a certain amount of interest. In social dancing you're asking for only three minutes of a person's time. It is a rare man or woman who's going to refuse such a modest request.

> **In social dancing you're asking for only three minutes of a person's time. It is a rare man or woman who's going to refuse such a modest request.**

My sister, Suzanne, has pointed out to me that some women are concerned that they will be considered overly aggressive if they ask a man to dance. I have to admit that this information took me completely by surprise, not only because I hadn't considered it, but because of the number of women who apparently share this concern. I was further taken aback when Suzanne told me that even she wasn't sure how men felt about this.

This issue seems to fall into one of those "differences between the sexes" questions that cause much confusion. In my opinion as a man, most men love to be asked to dance. I have to say "most men" because there are always those few who, for one reason or another, don't feel that way. There are also some women who don't want to dance with me because I'm not their "type" or I'm not up to their level of expertise. But these are the exceptions.

To repeat, most men love to be asked to dance. Asking is not considered aggressive behavior. A man considers it a compliment to his dancing ability, since male beginners are rarely asked to dance. As long as you let the man lead on the dance floor, he won't mind your asking him to dance with you. After the dance, compliment him on his ability to lead and he's yours for life. Flattery will get you on the dance floor every time!

If I'm making this sound too easy, I can't help it. It *is*

easy. But I also know how nervous some of us become merely thinking of asking a stranger to dance. It can be like having to give a speech to a small group of friends or colleagues. We know there is no reason to be afraid, but if you have a fear of public speaking, all the logic in the world is not going to help you feel more at ease until you break that fear and just do it.

This is another reason why going to a weekly dance is so important. Besides the obvious fact that it gives everyone more dance time, it also provides more opportunity for those of us who are on the shy side to get to know some of the regulars—the core group of people who attend week after week. Once you get to know a few people, it is easier to ask them to dance. The more dances you get, the more fun you have and the more people you get to meet and talk to. *Relationship building!* It's a pretty simple equation.

Following are some simple rules of etiquette to keep in mind. You will probably develop your own list as you go along, but this is a start.

MEN

Personal hygiene—I place this at the top of the list because virtually every dance instructor, as well as every woman I interviewed, mentioned this as a problem most often associated with men. You are dancing very, very closely to your partner in many of the social dances. If you have a breath or body odor problem, please do what is necessary to keep it in check. Many men bring a change of shirts to lessen a perspiration problem for a hot night with no air conditioning. Women do not appreciate having to place their hands on your sticky shoulder or back. If you had garlic for dinner, pop some mints in your mouth before the dance.

Escort the lady on and off the dance floor. Thank her

for the dance. This is good manners and will be greatly appreciated.

Be sensitive to how close your partner wants to dance. In many dances, this is dictated by the dance itself. As a general rule, most smooth-style ballroom dances necessitate a close partnering in order to execute the various moves properly. So, if you want to be joined at the waist, learn the tango. Rhythm dances tend to utilize a slightly more separate stance. Other dances, such as swing, are quite flexible with regard to proximity. Use your better judgment and don't make your partner feel unnecessarily uncomfortable.

> **Don't scan the room to find your next partner while you are dancing.**

Maintain eye contact. Don't scan the room to find your next partner while you are dancing.

Lead your partner. If she can't feel your lead, how can she follow?

Do not criticize. You asked her to dance, or she asked you. Neither of you asked for a dance lesson. As a beginner, it is unlikely you are in a position to be giving unsolicited advice. If, however, you feel you are the better dancer and there is a "problem," then it is your job to adjust. It is not your job because you are a man, but because it is always the responsibility of the better dancer to adjust. Consider altering your lead or your expectations.

If you are the victim of unwanted advice, you can politely suggest that "criticism ruins your concentration." It certainly will ruin mine. I've had this experience, and once something is said, you begin to second-guess everything you do for the rest of that dance. If the unwanted advice continues despite your request, it is reasonable to suggest (politely) to your partner that she is too good a dancer for someone of your skill level, and leave the dance floor.

Loud conversation, profanity, stamping the feet, writing on the wall, smoking tobacco, spitting or throwing anything on the floor, are strictly forbidden.
 —Thomas Hillgrove, *A Complete Practical Guide to the Art of Dancing*

WOMEN

Personal hygiene. This is as important for women as it is for men. There are few things that are more of a turn-off than poor hygiene. Also, if you have long hair, you may want to consider tying it back or up so that your partner doesn't get "whipped" during a turn or have trouble positioning his hand on your back.

Maintain eye contact. No one likes to dance with a partner who seems disinterested. Be relaxed and smile; it is fun you're having, right?

Follow your partner's lead. This is possibly the most important factor that makes a woman a good dancer, and a desired dance partner. As there is an art to leading, there is an art to following. Use every opportunity to hone your following skills. The biggest complaint a man has is when the lady tries to lead. Just as a man's ability to dance is judged greatly on his ability to communicate his intentions to his partner, a woman is similarly assessed on her responsiveness to the man's lead. Even if you feel the man is off the beat or not leading well, dance with him to his beat. **Refrain from leading!**

Let your partner escort you off the dance floor. Thank him for the dance. If you want to make sure he asks you again, compliment him on the way he executed a particular move, or one that he let you to execute.

> *Do not criticize. Neither of you asked for a dance lesson—only three minutes on the dance floor.*

Clothing. Consider your clothing choices in various dance positions so as to make sure they are appropriate.

Don't turn someone down and then dance with someone else. Unless the person was impolite, had poor personal hygiene, or was on a reality-altering substance, wait out a dance if you decline a man's request to trip the light fantastic. As you will discover if you choose to ask men to dance, it takes a certain amount of courage to do so. Bearing this in mind, you should accept at least one dance with a man who asks you to dance with him. You can always make some appropriate excuses should he ask you again, but at least you will have given him the courtesy of one dance, a favor you would appreciate, I'm sure, when the shoe is on the other foot.

Do not criticize. Neither of you asked for a dance lesson—only three minutes on the dance floor. If you happen to be in a dance class, and you think your partner requires assistance—not too unusual since men, as we've discussed, often begin at a disadvantage—remain silent. You are not the teacher.

Criticism can destroy the confidence of any beginner. If you are the recipient of unsolicited advice, you may want to suggest that public criticism makes you nervous. If your partner continues dishing it out anyway, you may want to excuse yourself from the dance floor, saying something like,

"You're just too good a dancer for me."

Any lady refusing to dance with a Gentleman, if disengaged,
will be under the penalty of not joining the two next Dances.
—G.M.S. Chivers, *A Pocket Companion to*
French and English Dancing

SAY WHAT?

What do you talk about once you're on the dance floor? Well, if you're anything like me, not much. Not because I can't think of anything to say, but because I can't think of two things at the same time. At least, I couldn't in the beginning. It was difficult enough keeping the rhythm. It's amazing how a simple question asked by your dance partner can interfere with your counting out the beats. This reminds me of the story about a woman leaving the dance floor at the end of a dance with a handsome stranger. Her friend, who had been watching with great interest, asked her what the man had been whispering in her ear while they danced. "Slow, slow, quick, quick," was her disappointed reply. Most dancers—men and women—have a good inner chuckle at this because we have all mentally done this at some time or another.

Men have the added responsibility of leading. That means we have to be thinking at least one step ahead, otherwise we give our partner some vague lead, thereby leaving it up to her to interpret what she thinks we want her to do. Of course, what she decides is not at all what *we* were thinking of. At this point we usually find ourselves standing in the middle of the dance floor, staring at each other. This can lead to some interesting dialogue, but it's not my favorite method of initiating a conversation.

Such miscues don't often happen to me any more, and I *can* hold a conversation with my partner—as long as it does-n't require too much thought and I'm not trying some new step. There are obviously an infinite number of subjects you can talk about while you dance. Anything related to dancing is, of course, a natural segue. Has he or she taken dance lessons or workshops? Where? With whom? What other styles of partner dancing are available nearby? That sort of thing. I would suggest you avoid asking questions that are too personal, controversial, or argumentative. People want to dance with other people who are cheerful and upbeat. Men should be careful with their jokes. If you want more suggestions, numerous books are available dedicated to the subjects of dating and/or conversation. *How to Find the Love of Your Life* by Ben Dominitz and *Conversationally Speaking* by Alan Garner are two that come to mind.

Dating can be controversial in itself. After all, what exactly is a date? This sounds like a simple enough question. But what happens if someone in the dance club wants to go with another member of the opposite sex to a dance or other social occasion? Or what if he or she would, as I mentioned earlier, like to get together for some practice? Such an innocent proposal might easily be misconstrued.

One dance class in Madison, Wisconsin, solved this quandary by introducing rules for "fetching." Fetching involves a "fetcher" and a "fetchee," with no specific gender being applied to either term. The fetcher does the asking, the fetchee does the accepting or rejecting. Without listing the actual rules involved, the idea, as I understand it, is to encourage dance members to invite other members to a dance event without any implications being attached to the request. Fetching, of course, can lead to dating, but dating is not an implicit next step. The term "fetching" is not a normal part of the social dancer's language, so I would avoid using it publicly, unless you wish to compliment someone, as in, "you look particularly 'fetching' this evening."

The fact that someone went through the trouble of

inventing fetching rules emphasizes the point that you will want to be careful about what you are asking and what is being accepted. For instance, if you are looking for someone to accompany you to a particular dance, you might ask him (or her) if he would be willing to be your "dance partner" for that evening. In doing so, you have provided at least a partial description of the role you desire of him and avoided the term "date," as well as a lengthy and potentially awkward description of what you don't want it to be (at least not yet). You have also defined the period of time—one evening. Sharing of expenses and other nebulous costs directly related to the "event" many need further clarification. Please remember, however, that it is

> **Don't be shortsighted and become disillusioned if you don't find the woman of your dreams at a dance. The woman in your dream may be your partner's sister or girlfriend.**

always proper etiquette to dance the first and last dance of the evening with the partner you arrive at the dance with.

Some women have told me they are reluctant to date men with whom they dance because if things don't work out they may feel awkward afterward. At the same time, these same women tell me their social lives have never been better. They are going out and doing different things with different people, all of which obviously increases their chances of meeting Mr. Right.

Remember what I said about expanding your horizons. What does it matter if you meet Mr. Right on the dance floor or on the golf course? The key is to build the relationships with people at the dance so these things can happen. This advice obviously applies to the men, as well. Don't be shortsighted and become disillusioned if you don't find the woman of your dreams at a dance. The woman in your dream may be your partner's sister or girlfriend.

Skippy Blair wrote a short article for West Coast Swing dancers that contained a list of suggestions and comments regarding dance relationships. Since this list is equally appropriate for social dancers of all kinds, I include it here (with Skippy's permission) so that you may refer to it as you progress through the learning curve. I hope you find it helpful.

RELATIONSHIPS
All You Ever Need to Know
Can Be Learned in a West Coast Swing Class
Skippy Blair © 3/95 rev. 1/96

1. Lead her *gently* and she'll follow you anywhere. For every *action* there is an equal and opposite *reaction*.
2. Never *criticize* a Partner. The only person you can fix is *you*. (The person who is responsible for making an *adjustment* is the one who knows an adjustment needs to be made.)
3. A Lead is an *indication* of direction (a suggestion, not a *demand*).
4. A *partnership* in today's society is 50/50. Both partners are equally responsible for the outcome of the partnership.
5. If either one of us insists on deciding who is *right* and who is *wrong*, we *both* lose.
6. The *first rule* in learning something new is—Don't Hurt Anybody.
7. Be sensitive to your Partner. Never blame or ridicule. You can make it right (don't adjust the Partner—adjust you).
8. Always concentrate on *what* is right rather than *who* is right.
9. *Teamwork* gets the most points. You are judged by how good you make your partner look.

10. A good partnership requires Patience, Understanding, and an Awareness of the needs of the partner. Stay focused.
11. The way to help a partner improve, is to do your part so well that you know that you are not part of the problem.
12. Life is a *joy* when we're both in step to the same *beat.*
13. Praise works wonders. Applaud little accomplishments and bigger accomplishments will follow.
14. We frequently judge others, not by who they are, but by who we are when we are with them. Make your partner feel wonderful.
15. Every dance is a Three Minute Relationship. If someone can't complete one whole dance without criticism, it is highly probable that when the music stops, the criticism won't. *Run!*
16. A successful Partnership maintains the separate uniqueness of each individual, without disrupting the connection of the partnership.

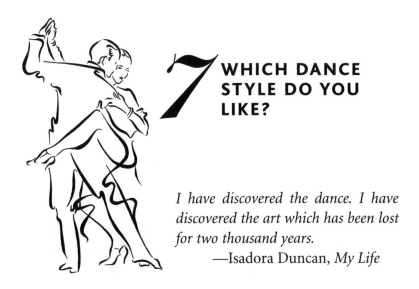

7 WHICH DANCE STYLE DO YOU LIKE?

I have discovered the dance. I have discovered the art which has been lost for two thousand years.
    —Isadora Duncan, *My Life*

BALLROOM

Paul Grecki, who teaches ballroom dancing as well as the Lindy, has found that women (pay attention guys!) have a lot of interest in smooth style dances such as the fox trot, waltz, and tango. A smooth dance is any dance that progresses around the floor. Many women, according to Paul, come into the studio saying that they want to look elegant, referring to the "look" associated with these types of dances.

Others prefer the passion and rhythm of the Latin dances. Rhythm dances—except for the samba—are danced in place, usually in a small square or circle. Examples of rhythm dances are salsa and mambo, rumba, cha-cha, samba, and merengue.

Here are some brief descriptions of the more popular ballroom dances. Tempos are provided in both measures per minute (MPM) and beats per minute (BPM). The tempos give you an idea of the relative speed, or pace, of the each dance. It can also help when you choose music for practice.

I have also characterized each dance as Level One, Two, Three, or Four, based on Skippy Blair's system. She rates each dance with regard to the music and movement involved, and the accompanying degree of difficulty. Dances may often encompass more than one level of difficulty. West Coast Swing, for example, is a Level Three dance. However, it can be taught up to Level Five, but it can also be taught well and understood well at Level Two—the level I have ascribed to it. The mambo, however, requires subtle body ripples even at the basic level, making it a Level Four dance.

The level I have assigned to each dance is the lowest level at which the dance can be both *taught and understood well.* These levels are far from being universally accepted, and many dance instructors will, I'm certain, disagree. I have included them as a general guideline, so that you have some idea as to the relative difficulty of the various dances.

SMOOTH STYLE

The music often contains string instruments, giving it a full-bodied sound.

Fox trot: Founded by Harry Fox in 1913 as part of his vaudeville act, this is one of the all-time favorite ballroom dances. It is also a foundation dance. Very smooth and graceful; think of Fred Astaire and Ginger Rogers. A dance of love; the kind of mature love one experiences after marriage.
Tempo: 28-37 MPM; 112-148 BPM
Level One

Waltz: The oldest ballroom dance and the first dance where the man actually held the woman in his arms. Very romantic—a courting dance. One is often reminded of life's happier moments. The slow tempo and repetitive rhythm make it an easy dance to learn. Sometimes referred to as "the last dance," the waltz is commonly seen at weddings and other celebrations, and is often the final dance of the evening.
Tempo: 28-36 MPM; 84-108 BPM
Level Two

Viennese Waltz: A fast-paced, beautiful dance character-ized by elegance and charm.

Tempo: 50-60 MPM; 150-180 BPM
Level Three/Four

Tango: The dance of love. Very pas-sionate—the man and woman dance so closely! Originated with the lower classes of Buenos Aires where it as much a religion as a dance. Its fiery passion and sensuality reflect the passionate, exciting music. There are different styles of tango, each of which has its own per-sonality. Barbara Garvey, in "Return of the Tango," *The Smithsonian Magazine,* September 1993, noted that:

> "The tango is like stages of a marriage. The American Modern Tango is like the beginning of a love affair, when you are both very romantic and on your best behavior."

"The tango is like stages of a marriage. The American Modern Tango is like the beginning of a love affair, when you are both very romantic and on your best behavior. The Argentine Tango is when you are in the heat of things and all kinds of emotions are flying: passion, anger, humor. The International Standard Tango is like the end of the marriage, when you are staying together for the sake of the children."

The basic steps of the American Modern Tango are easy to learn. Sometimes referred to as a *Latin fox trot,* it is known for its leg wraps and hip circles. Many of the advanced levels of performance are found in the Argentine Tango.

Tempo: 32-34 MPM; 128-136 BPM
Level Two (American Tango)

Quickstep: A fun, letting-loose kind of dance. Fast fox trot. The New York style is sometimes referred to as the Peabody.

Tempo: 54-64 MPM; 216-256 BPM
Level Four

LATIN

The music styles often have more percussion instruments. There can also be slow ballads as in rumba.

> "The Argentine Tango is when you are in the heat of things and all kinds of emotions are flying: passion, anger, humor. The International Standard Tango is like the end of the marriage, when you are staying together for the sake of the children."

Rumba: Queen of Latin American dances. Slow and sensuous, this is a dance of love with a Latin rhythm. The emphasis is on the lady, with the man chasing her. It's a dance of "cat and mouse." She is all the while enticing him, but never quite lets him catch her. The basic steps are very simple. Perfecting them, however, can take years. The rumba can be danced in place (on the spot) on a crowded dance floor.
Tempo: 28-34 MPM; 112-136 BPM
Level One

Cha-cha: A Cuban dance with staccato rhythm. One of the most popular South American dances. Similar to the rumba, but slightly quicker and more playful. A dance of flirtation. The man will likely catch the woman. Danced in a square space.
Tempo: 26-33 MPM; 104-132 BPM
Level Three, although it can be taught at Level Two as well.

Samba: Brazilian dance. The waltz with hiccups. A party dance—think of Mardi Gras. The step patterns resemble disco basic and are very easy to learn, but the rhythmic lilt required to give this dance its distinctive look makes it difficult to perfect.
Tempo: 48-58 MPM; 96-116 BPM
Level Four

Mambo: Means "voodoo princess" in Haitian Creole. A fusion of Swing and Cuban rumba. Danced with a pronounced hip movement to fast music with a heavy beat. A sexy, very seductive dance. Earthy.
Tempo: 40-51 MPM; 160-204 BPM
Level Four

Salsa: This dance is all about emotion; it is danced with the heart. Although it shares many of the basic moves with the mambo, the feel of the dance is different. Turns are an important, integral part of salsa. The percussion instruments (bongos and maracas) give salsa music its rhythm.
Tempo: 40-51 MPM; 160-204 BPM
Level One

(Note: Some people refer to salsa and mambo interchangeably. There are different styles of salsa, and it is often *salsa suave* that is confused with the mambo. They have similar patterns as well as a similar look, but an entirely different feeling. The elegance and delightful posturing of salsa is very different from the wild abandon of the mambo.)

Merengue: (Me-rren-gay) The national dance of the Dominican Republic. Sometimes referred to as "the Thief" because its foot patterns were stolen from other dances. Fun. Casual (bare feet or sandals) or sophisticated, depending on your mood and the music. Very popular and adaptable, it can be danced to genuine merengue music as well as current chart hits. Smooth, and very easy to learn. If you can walk, you can merengue.
Tempo: 29-32 MPM; 116-128 BPM
Level One

CONTRA

Contra dances are among the least formal and most social of all the dances. Contra dancers are the cross-country skiers of life—friendly, low key, budget-minded, and family oriented. They come from all walks of life, often have a potluck dinner before or during the dance, and hang out with the musicians afterwards. A caller, who works with a group of live musicians, teaches each dance before it is actually performed to the music, then narrates the dance so each dancer can perform each movement to the music. Partners are arranged in circles that rotate partners between circles so that in all but the largest events each participant will have danced with virtually every other participant by the end of the evening. I have only attended two contra dances, and because of the extraordinary amount of turning and twirling, I got extremely dizzy both times and had to bow out. I'm told that the secret to avoiding this problem is to always look into your partner's eyes.

Contra dances continue to be extremely popular around the country, and the people, as I indicated, are exceptionally sociable. I suggest giving one a try if for no other reason than just for the experience.

Some people march to a different drummer—and some people polka.
—Los Angeles Times Syndicate

> **Contra dancers are the cross-country skiers of life—friendly, low key, budget-minded, and family oriented.**

COUNTRY WESTERN

Country western dancing usually consists of three or four types of dance: the Texas two-step, line dancing, waltzes, and polkas.

Line dancing is obviously not a partner-style dance, and my own opinion of it until recently was that it was just another type of freestyle dance. I was dead set against it because the last thing in the world I wanted was to go back to freestyle dancing again, especially when I could partner dance with a woman.

Then I talked to Sherry Palencia, a well-known C/W dance instructor in our area. Sherry pointed out that one of the main advantages of line dancing is that it creates a feeling of friendliness and familiarity among the participants. After you've been doing it a while, you get to know the people around you so that when a Texas two-step occurs, you're already at ease with one another. It's not a question of, "Oh, will anyone ask me to dance?" You just turn around and say, "Hey Bill (or Donna, Laura, etc.), let's two-step!" (This presupposes that you have learned the Texas two-step.)

> ... one of the main advantages of line dancing is that it creates a feeling of friendliness and familiarity among the participants.

In this scenario, line dancing becomes a form of introduction to another type of dance. So I can see the benefits that line dancing has to offer as a means of breaking the ice.

Country western is done in bars and restaurants, as well as in dance halls across the country. Because line dancing takes up a lot of room, you'll usually find C/W dancing in an establishment with a large dance floor. The music has evolved over the last ten years, so if you haven't been to one of these dances recently, give it a try. You certainly shouldn't have any trouble finding a dance in your area, and I can guarantee you won't be alone.

SWING

All swing dances share a common rhythm. This is what

places different forms of swing under the same umbrella. Professional dance instructor Skippy Blair has listed the following forms of dance in the generic family of swing: Lindy, New Yorker, Dallas Push, Houston Whip, Imperial Swing, Carolina shag, East Coast Swing, and West Coast Swing.

Below are more complete descriptions of three of these: the Lindy, the Carolina shag, and West Coast Swing.

Lindy: (Lindy Hop, East Coast Swing, or Jitterbug) This is the granddaddy of the swing dances. Named after Charles Lindbergh's solo across the Atlantic, it is one of the most popular of the partner-style dances. You may have seen it performed in movies such as *A League of Our Own, Swing Kids,* or while watching the clothing commercials for The Gap with the dancers performing aerial moves.

The Lindy Hop began in the 1920s and 30s in the dance clubs in New York City and was one of the last partner dances before rock and roll and the twist exploded onto the scene. One of the clubs was called the Savoy; hence, another name, Savoy-style Lindy. This is one of the more popular styles of Lindy being danced today. There is a great deal of confusion concerning the differences between the Lindy, East Coast Swing, and the jitterbug. (The term "jitterbug" is said to have been coined when a commentator, watching a Lindy Hop competition, exclaimed, "Look at those jitterbuggers." The name stuck.)

The confusion centers on the patterns. There are disagreements as to which dances have 6-beat patterns and which have 8-beat patterns. East Coast Swing instructors usually begin with 6-beat patterns, Lindy instructors with 8-beat. In the final analysis, however, every form of swing dancing uses both 6-beat and 8-beat forms. Or, to paraphrase Frankie Manning, if you're dancing to swing music, you're *swingin'.* And that's good enough for me. One caveat, though. Find out what type of swing—6-beat rhythm or 8-beat rhythm—is being danced at the venue you plan to attend on a regular basis. Then make sure that the instructor or studio you choose teaches that style.

The Lindy has become popular among all ages once again—college students and retirees alike. It has especially taken hold with people age 20 through 40, so you shouldn't have much trouble finding a dance club nearby.

New bands are popping up and playing new versions of the original music, but the rhythm is the same as that found in Duke Ellington's "It Don't Mean a Thing if It Ain't Got That Swing" and Elvis Presley's "Blue Suede Shoes." If you like the music, you'll love the dance!

> **Shag . . . is not just a dance, it's a lifestyle. It's party and play. It's where little boys meet the Queen of the Hop. As one shagger puts it, "If I hadn't learned this dance, I'd still be a virgin."**

Tempo: 140-184 BPM (This is approximate only. Many of today's dance tunes are considerably faster. Lindy tempos are nearly always given in BPM.)

Level Two

Carolina shag: The shag is the Carolina state dance. Shag, however, is not just a dance, it's a lifestyle. It's party and play. It's where little boys meet the Queen of the Hop. As one shagger puts it, "If I hadn't learned this dance, I'd still be a virgin."

Shag is a slowed-down, smoother version of the jitterbug with very little hand motion and more intricate footwork. This focus on the footwork is most likely the reason many female shaggers wear slacks.

Each year, the Society of Stranders (S.O.S.) hosts what

are undoubtedly the two largest adult beach parties in the world at Myrtle Beach, South Carolina—the Spring Safari and the Fall Migration. These events are attended by 10,000+ members, so you may want to plan a trip down there to check it out. Perhaps you'll make some new friends. Then you'll have an excuse to go back year after year—to visit old friends.

West Coast Swing is the official state dance of California. A close relative of the Lindy, swing dancers sometimes refer to WCS as the "Dancer's Dance."

Tempo: 115-150 BPM
Level Two

West Coast Swing: West Coast Swing is the official state dance of California. A close relative of the Lindy, swing dancers sometimes refer to WCS as the "Dancer's Dance." Skippy Blair makes the case that WCS is an educated dance requiring a 50/50 partnership. The follower needs to know as much about the dance as the leader, since she is not just mirroring her partner. This allows the woman to be creative and independent, yet still remain connected to her partner, who sets the tone of the dance. These characteristics make WCS somewhat more complex and difficult to learn. The dance's style and grace, combined with a certain sultriness and sensuality, make it an extremely popular dance.

The sensuality of the dance is not the only reason for its popularity. WCS can accommodate all but the most eclectic tastes in music, traversing the spectrum from blues and R&B to Madonna. For many, WCS has become a way of life. Perhaps it will become yours.

Tempo: 28-36 MPM; 112-144 BPM
Level Two

8 WHAT TO WEAR

"I want a blue dress," I told him. "A pure blue with no green in it at all. Like the blue you find in the paintings of Monet. I would love the dress to be made of satin with myriads of ostrich feathers, low in the back and high in the front."
—Ginger Rogers

"I love to watch people come to country western class for the first time, especially the men," says Sherry Palencia.

"The first night the dancer has the red kerchief, the boots, even the handkerchief hanging out of the back pocket to wipe the sweat from his brow. He hasn't done a step yet. But he's got the handkerchief to wipe it off."

Ballroom and swing dancers are often just the opposite. They start off wearing their normal street clothes and before long they'll be toting in their shoe bag with umpteen pairs of dance shoes and a special wire brush to clean their suede soles, along with any other dance paraphernalia they feel may be needed.

This is particularly true for women because of the tremendous variety of dancewear available. Shoes, for example. For men, the choice is pretty simple. Soles: leather or suede. Color: black, unless you opt for the more eye-catching two-tone brown and white, in which case you had better be able to dance up to the expectations demanded of someone wearing such apparel. That's about the extent of your choice, without getting into the quality of the shoe.

Compare this with the options available for women. Soles: leather or suede. Color: every color of the rainbow and then some. Type: open toe, closed toe, criss-cross, ankle straps, T-straps, one-inch heels, two-inch heels, three-inch heels, plus half sizes. Dress or casual. Shoes for slippery floors and for sticky ones. That's just the shoes.

As a bachelor, I have to admit that I had no idea of the time and effort women put into choosing what to wear until I walked into my sister's house one day to find her modeling a new dance skirt for her daughter. As I can best describe it, the skirt consisted primarily of strips of black material hanging from her waist. I asked Sue where she happened to find this skirt, since I knew she had been searching for some time. She informed me she had found a dress whose skirt she had been looking for, so she purchased it and cut everything off above the waist! Then she cut pieces of the material and attached them to the bottom portion of what had once been another dress.

I looked again at the (almost) final product and decided that there couldn't have been much to the lower part to begin with since there wasn't a whole lot there now, including the strips.

My sister and her daughter were meticulously and intently studying this result to make sure there were enough strips to cover the bare necessities and that they (the strips) were long enough to create interest but not appear inappropriate.

Inappropriate, by the way, is defined differently on the dance floor than in public. Sue performed various spins and twirls to make sure the skirt created the desired effect. Finally, after seemingly torturous deliberation, they decided it met all the necessary criteria. That, of course, didn't stop them from modifying it further before the actual dance.

For women readers, perhaps none of this is new to you. For me, however, this was the beginning of a learning experience.

Especially when Sue informed me she had to go find the right color underpants to match her skirt. At that point I decided it was time to leave. I was finding out more about my sister than I wanted to know.

Most women do want to create one smooth look which means using their hose to tie their dance briefs and shoes together, which also gives the effect of elongating the leg. This is easy to accomplish by matching the color of the hose with the briefs and shoes—for example, black dance briefs, black hose and shoes. Dark shoes with pale hose, on the other hand, would cut the leg line at the ankle, appearing to shorten the leg.

New dancers should dress differently than experienced ones. Just as two-tone shoes on a beginning male dancer are a potential source of humor, a female novice would be inviting similar stares should she be wearing a racy costume more appropriate for the woman that can dance up to the *attitude* required of such attire. You can still dress elegantly; just be certain you take a good look in the mirror first to make sure it's the image you want to present.

When all is said and done, being comfortable in what you wear is best. Use common sense and dress appropriately and you shouldn't get into too much trouble.

One note of caution to women. As your arm travels upward during an overhead spin, likewise does your shirt or blouse. Be careful with those short tops that show off your midriff. During a double spin, you could be showing off a lot more than you anticipated. If in doubt, try it at home first. Once you are on the dance floor, it's too late.

SHOES

The most important part of your gear is a comfortable pair of shoes. Whether you're dancing ballroom, swing, country western, shag, or anything else, if your feet are in pain you won't enjoy the experience.

Be sure to break in the new pair at home or while practicing, or at least bring a comfortable pair with you if your feet get tired from the new shoes.

The most important part of your gear is a comfortable pair of shoes. Whether you're dancing ballroom, swing, country western, shag, or anything else, if your feet are in pain you won't enjoy the experience.

Carol Fournier of Toe to Toe Dance Shoes offers the following advice for proper fit and care of dance shoes:

"For ultimate comfort, dance shoes should feel "snug like a glove" without pinching any part of your foot. The recommended fit for an open-toed ladies' sandal should allow the end of your toes to fall from within a half-inch of, to slightly hanging over, the end of the shoe. For closed-toe shoes, we usually look for the end of the toes to be approximately one-half-inch to three-quarters-inch from the end of the shoes so as not to crush the toes.

"To check the width of the shoe, we usually like to ensure that you are pressing against the sides of the shoe while standing (thus no excess leather fabric), without any portion of your foot feeling crushed, as a shoe will stretch as it is worn. Remember, *snug like a glove* is the key.

"For shoes which lace, it is important to have a small-to-medium gap in the lace so as to accommodate stretching. If a shoe stretches too much, you can use a tongue pad to take up the slack in the lacing. Place the self-adhesive tongue pad on the underside of the tongue. Another recommendation for keeping a shoe fitting snug is to add a metatarsal pad to the bottom of the shoe. This will take up the slack and allow the foot to fill the shoe again.

"For a good fitting dance shoe, try not to have any gap in the back of the heel. However, occasionally this can't be avoided in a person with a broader metatarsal area and a "narrow" heel. In this situation, the recommendation is to get a heel grip, which you can purchase in many drugstores or shoe repair shops.

"Two different size feet? Because it is so important that a dance shoe fit well, we suggest you look for a dance shoe company that will make two different sizes as "a pair." The additional charge, which should not exceed 15% of the cost, is a small price to pay for comfort. The shoes must be "made to order," otherwise the color and texture of the leathers may not match.

"All good dance shoes have a few things in common. First, they should have a steel shank to support your foot and keep your arch from "flattening" as you dance. Second, dance shoes should have soles created for the specific type of dancing you are doing. Chrome suede bottoms reduce the friction on the dance floor, allowing you to move more easily. Reducing the friction should also help reduce the fatigue in your joints. Rubber soles are used on shoes for Lindy Hop. Lindy hoppers prefer to know that their feet will be firmly planted on the floor when they come down from jumps and lifts.

"Cushioning is also important. Cushioning minimizes foot shock and whole body stress, enabling you to enjoy dancing more comfortably and for longer periods. Dance shoes should be designed with natural foot and toe shapes, to help minimize undue pressure, and distortion of toe and metatarsal bones.

All good dance shoes have a few things in common. First, they should have a steel shank to support your foot and keep your arch from "flattening" as you dance. Second, dance shoes should have soles created for the specific type of dancing you are doing.

"Women will find they are more secure in a dance shoe than in street wear. Dance shoes have T-straps, ankle wraps, laces or elastic to keep them snug and secure on your feet. I personally found I was curling my toes in an effort to keep my street shoes on my feet while dancing. I've even "thrown a shoe," as have many others, while dancing and had to retrieve it from across the floor. The confidence you gain from knowing you are not going to have to stop in the middle of the dance to hobble across the floor in one shoe to retrieve the one that flew across the room is invaluable.

"To care for your shoes, it is recommended that you brush the suede soles with a steel brush to prevent dust and dance wax from building up on the soles, which should be kept dry. For this reason, dancers carry their dance shoes in a shoe bag to their dance location, and then change shoes. You should periodically apply a cream leather polish to keep the leather supple and healthy. For patent leather shoes, consider carrying a little Vaseline with you, as a "real" non-synthetic patent will stick to the other shoe if they happen to touch or brush against one another. Apply the Vaseline minimally to the inside areas were you shoes could potentially touch."

CLOTHES FOR DANCING BALLROOM STYLES

The trouble with nude dancing is that not everything stops when the music stops.
> —Robert Helpmann, regarding
> Broadway musical *Oh Calcutta*

Ballroom styles are, as you probably imagine, the most elegant of the dances. When Paul Grecki said that women come into the studio saying they want to feel elegant, that could in most cases apply to the clothing as well. When ballroom dancing, you always want to look nice. That usually means black shoes with suede bottoms for men and one-inch to three-inch heels, again with suede soles, for women.

For general ballroom dancing, a shirt and slacks for the man are fine; a dress or skirt with a slightly full cut for the woman. If you are planning to wear a long evening dress, make sure that you are not going to step on the skirt when you move backwards.

For Latin dancing, Patti Panebianco, a ballroom Latin champion, recommends high-waisted pants for men. This tends to show off the hip action in the Latin dances and offers a treat to the ladies. For women, Mindy Aloff of the *New York Times* recommends dresses or skirts that "go as high as the cellulite allows, and they tend either to be spandex-tight or cut so the skirt swirls out in a flat turn like an LP record." Whatever you choose, Patti recommends that you feel good in what you wear and leave the ostrich feathers, beads, and rhinestones at home, except for competition when you want to add flair and elegance. They may have worked for Fred and Ginger, but if you've ever had the misfortune to slip on one of those beads or gems, you know that what works in the movies doesn't translate so well into real life.

CLOTHES FOR CONTRA DANCING

As I mentioned earlier, contra dancers are the cross-country skiers of the dance world. They have their own particular style, which emphasizes comfort and practicality. Since there is often no air conditioning in the dance hall, dancers do not hesitate to wear shorts in the summertime. The exceptionally friendly atmosphere, however, more than makes up for the lack of modern conveniences. Since there's very little footwork in contra dance, ordinary soft-soled footwear is fine. Tennis shoes are perfectly acceptable.

CLOTHES FOR COUNTRY WESTERN DANCING

According to Sherry Palencia, all you need is a comfortable pair of shoes. And comfortable may not mean a pair of cowboy boots, unless you have a pair that you sleep in. For regular dances, the western shirt is optional. If you want, you can save that for the Saturday night dance when the band is playing and you want your best western look. Jeans do seem to be the standard, though, at least for men. For the woman, once she gets away from the peach button shirt and the unisex outfit, it's a skirt or jeans. Again, the real western clothes don't come out of the closet until the Saturday night dance.

SHAG CLOTHING

Proper shag attire may vary according to geography. Norfleet Jones, a shag Hall of Famer, says that all a man needs is a shirt, slacks, and a pair of Bass Wiggins or Cole-Hanns—penny loafers to those in other parts of the country—and he's ready to hit the dance floor. Flats to heels are acceptable for the ladies, and slacks preferable to skirts and dresses. Competitive dancers will opt for suede soles.

SWING DANCE CLOTHING

It's more straightforward for the guys, although that's beginning to change. It used to be that we would start off with either street shoes or sneakers (sneakers stick and make it difficult to pivot) and eventually capitulate and get ourselves a pair of dance shoes with suede bottoms. And that was the extent of it.

Now, depending on your age, taste, geographic location, and style of swing, men have almost as many options as women. If you're younger and dancing the Lindy, you may be wearing a Zoot suit, with pegged pants and padded shoulders.

If you're dancing to West Coast Swing, it's less dramatic,

with the style dictated somewhat by which coast you are on, or the nearest city. The West Coast seems to be a little flashier than the East.

In the end, it comes down to your shoes: leather soles on tile floors, or barroom floors that tend to get liquid spilled on them; suede soles for wooden floors and ease of movement; rubber soles if you're doing aerial moves and require stability, and have knees that can put up with the strain. The rest of your attire is going to be dictated, to some extent, by where you are going that night. Your best jeans are not going to make it at the Supper Club in Manhattan.

Footwear is the primary focus for women as well. I've seen everything from sneakers and saddle shoes to elegant footwear at our weekly dances. Two-inch heels will probably be your limit when it comes to your footwear (add a half to one inch if you live on the West Coast). Anything higher will most likely be too uncomfortable, not to mention extremely dangerous. Suede soles are recommended.

It used to be that dancewear for women didn't get much fancier than skirts and blouses at these events. However, as the popularity of swing dancing has increased, so have the variations in clothing styles. Vintage clothing is extremely popular among the Lindy Hoppers right now, making such clothing less accessible and therefore more expensive. West Coast Swing has a more current look—check your nearest dance club to see what's acceptable.

A night on the town does, of course, put more of a premium on elegance. Your attire, to a large extent, is dictated by your destination.

I want one word on my tombstone—dancer.
                    —Agnes DeMille, *U.S. News & World Report*

ONE LAST WORD

You should now be ready to enter the world of social dancing and enjoy its numerous joys and benefits—better health and fitness, greater self-confidence, and increased popularity.

It is my hope that dance will become a passion for you and not something that you take out of the closet and brush off for special occasions such as weddings and anniversary parties. If you set aside just one night a week for dancing, I'm sure that you will find yourself meeting more persons of the opposite sex, developing a multitude of new relationships, and enjoying a newfound popularity that will add excitement and zest to your life. In short, I believe that dancing can go a long way toward making you a happier person.

I'D LIKE TO HEAR FROM YOU

I would very much like to know how partner dancing has changed your social life. What obstacles did you have to overcome and how did you do it? Have you found romance? You may have some interesting and humorous stories to tell. Most social dancers do. Perhaps you can be in my next book.

You may write to me at Sundance Publishing Inc, P.O. Box 932, Patchogue, New York 11772-0932. Or email me at: **Craig@Sundancepublishing.net.**

Now, go out and hit the "wood"!

RESOURCE GUIDE

DANCE CLOTHES

Back Bay Dancewear
800-554-2340
www.backbaydancewear.com
Email: dance@xensei.com
Practice clothes, custom dresses, men's pants and shirts, CDs and videos.
Free catalog.

The Ballroom Shoppe
2737 E. Oakland Park Blvd.,
Suite 201
Ft. Lauderdale, FL 33306
954-564-7176
Fax: 954-564-9075
Dance clothes, shoes.
Catalog available.

Dancepants
100 Buckingham Dr. #101
Santa Clara, CA 95051
408-345-7089
Email: www.dancepants.com

Dance Vision
8933 W. Sahara Blvd.
Las Vegas, NV 89117
800-851-2813
Fax: 702-256-4227
Email: info@dancevision.com

Discount Dance Supply
1401 S. Village Way
Santa Ana, CA 92705
800-328-7107
www.discdance.com

Jodee Adair
P.O. Box 10440
Santa Ana, CA 92711
714-282-1318
800-70-JODEE
Special clothes, swing pants.

DANCE SHOES

Back Bay Dancewear
800-554-2340
www.backbaydancewear.com
Email: dance@xensei.com
Practice clothes, custom dresses, men's pants and shirts, CDs and videos.
Free catalog.

Carmen's Dance Shoes
6506 El Cajon Blvd., Suite D
San Diego, CA 92115
800-854-4318 or 619-287-5787
www.carmensdanceshoes.com

Champion Dance Shoes
3383 Barham Blvd.
Los Angeles, CA 90068
800-40-DANCE or
323-874-8704
www.championdanceshoes.com
Distributor for fine quality dance shoes such as Werner Kern, Dance Art by Diamont, and others. Also offers dance accessories, including Ballroom and Latin CDs.

Coast Ballroom Shoes
13401 Saticoy Street
North Hollywood, CA 91605
818-786-0717
Fax: 818-786-1227

**Constantine Celebrity
Ballroom Dance Shoes**
15110 Stone Ridge Trace
Minneapolis, MN 55391
612-476-0058

Dance Distributors
P.O. Box 11440
Harrisburg, PA 17108
800-33-DANCE

Dancehappy.com
P.O. Box 7678
Phoenix, AZ 85013
602-222-6666
www.dancehappy.com
Ballroom and swing dance
shoes and accessories.

Discount Dance Supply
1401 S. Village Way
Santa Ana, CA 92705
800-328-7107
www.discdance.com

GAMBA USA
209 S. High Street
Lobby Annex
Columbus, OH 43215
614-463-1080
Fax: 614-463-1078

Parti-Time Dance Shoes
439 George Cross
Norman, OK 73069
800-354-3101 or 405-321-4468

SavoyStyle Swing Dance Shop
32101 Ellison Way
Fort Bragg, CA 95437
888-507-2869

Fax: 707-964-4473
www.swingdanceshop.com
Bleyer's swing dance shoes.

Showtime Dance Shoes
Mail Order Division
3571 Chamblee Tucker Road
Atlanta, GA 30341
800-433-5541
www.dancescape.com/
showtime
Email:
info.paradise@dancescape.com

Stardust Dance Supplies Ltd.
92 Brookland Dr.
Brampton, Ontario L6T 3G6
Canada
888-793-7681
www.stardust-shoes.com
Email: stan@stardust-shoes.com

Stonybird Dance Shoes
71 Soledad Drive
Monterey, CA 93940
831-648-8725
Email: stoneybird@aol.com
Dance shoes.

SUPADANCE USA
398 N.E. 6th Ave.
Delray Beach, FL 33483
800-888-5429 or 407-265-0697

Toe to Toe Dance Shoes
5522 Old Franklin Road
Grand Blanc, MI 48439
800-484-5431 PIN 5732 or
810-695-1010
www.toe2toe.com

Zee Dancing Shoes
P.O. Box 30793
North Las Vegas, NV 89036
702-438-4401

INTERNET SITES

5678 Magazine
www.5678magazine.com
Source for dance teachers, events, places to dance, swing, country, ballroom, and more. Includes feature articles from the magazine.

Ballroom Dance Competition Calendar
Possibly the most complete site for ballroom competition schedules. The web site is currently under construction, so check the United States Amateur Ballroom Dancers Association site for details (www.usabda.org).

Betty B's Bungalow
Http://users.vnet.net/bbhunt/intro1.html
Articles on shag dancing. Also has a Shagger's Play List sampler containing different types of shag music.

Bob's Contra Dance Pages
www.voicenet.com/~squeeze/contras.html
Contra dance and related links, general dance information, dance festivals, and lists of dances by state.

CDSS (Country Dance and Song Society, Inc.)
www.cdss.org
132 Main Street
P.O. Box 338
Haydenville, MA 01039
Contact: Pat MacPherson
413-268-7426
Email: sales@cdss.org
Source of information for people interested in folk-related dances such as contra dance. Members receive a bi-monthly newsletter. An annual directory, books and recordings, as well as a list of instructors are available. CDSS also organizes summer dance camps for adults and families.

Charlie Seelig's Contra Dance Links for the US, Canada, and the World
www.tiac.net/users/cseelig/contra/contralinks.shtml
Large set of links to contra dancing pages.

Dance Magic
www.dancemagic.com
Videocassettes for ballroom, latin, C/W.

Dance Plus
www.danceplus.com
Ballroom dance supply company that sells strict-time ballroom dance CDs out of Canada.

Dance Store
www.dancestore.com
410-990-0009
Swing dance shoes, clothes, videos & CDs. Great selection of Lindy videos.

Dance Vision
www.dancevision
Videotapes, dance fashions, shoes, jewelry, CDs, books, and dance camps.

DanceArt.com
Dance chat forum.

DanceDanceDance
www.dancedancedance.com/
swingclubs1.html
List of dance clubs and organizations alphabetized by state.

Dancers at Sea
www.dancersatsea.com.
Dance cruises catering to both singles and couples.

The Dancers CD Store
www.cwo.com/~bcdancer/
cds.html
References to pages or lists of ballroom and swing music.

DJ "G" Parmerton
www.musicfordancing.com/
top10/
DJ "G" Parmerton's Top 10 West Coast Swing songs.

Dwayne Johnson's Contra Dance Map
HTTP://ourworld.compuserve.com/homepage/
D_Johnson
An attempt to link every known contra web site in the US and Canada.

Henry's Dance Hotlist
http://zeus.ncsa.uiuc.edu:8080/
~hneeman/dance_hotlist.html
Extensive listing of dance pages on the Web, including swing, ballroom, Argentine tango, salsa, and C/W.

Lindy Hop Links
www.panix.com/~vannevar/
swing.htm
Links to Lindy Hop-related

internet sites.

The New England Swing Dance Server
www.javanet.com/~stefan/
dance/ne_swing.html
Swing dance events in both the NE area and nationally. Other dance links as well.

The New York Swing Dance Server
www.nyswingdance.com
This site not only contains a great deal of information about the New York swing dance scene, but it can also get you to many useful swing dance-related sites.

Rec.Arts.Dance (FAQ)
www.eijkhout.net/rad/
index3.html
Links to information about many different types of dance.

Raper's Dance Corner
www.raper.com/dance/
Possibly the largest site on the web related to swing dance. Contains information on swing and C/W dance, clubs & associations, music & dance videos, dance therapy, and more. A lot of useful information here. Also links to related topics.

Shag Atlanta's Shag Dance Server
www.shagatlanta.com
Club list, party calendar, shag dance instructors, membership information, and more. Also lists top 40 shag songs.
Hotline: 678-442-6457

SOS (Society of Stranders)
www.shagdance.com
List of shag clubs, dance contests, music, parties, and events.

Stefan Gonick's West Coast Swing Music Recommendations
www.javanet.com/~stefan/dance/music.html
West Coast Swing music recommendations.

Swingset.net
www.swingset.net
Daily update of the swing scene in CA, NY, Chicago, and Las Vegas. Information on where to go for dance lessons, plus schedules for your favorite swing bands. This site even helps you find a dance partner.

Total Swing
www.totalswing.com
Articles, music, calendar, and what's new in swing dance.

United States Amateur Ballroom Dancers Association (USABDA)
www.usabda.org
Ballroom dance events, magazines, local chapter listings, youth college network.

World Swing Dance Council (WSDC)
www.swingdancecouncil.com
List of national events, swing dance instructors, plus other recommended dance links. Also includes a Competitors Registry and a Members Registry.

Yahoo's Ballroom Dancing Index
www.yahoo.com/arts/performing_arts/dance/ballroom
Wealth of information on clubs, dances, videos.

Yehoodi
www.yehoodi.com
Swing dance news, videos, and NY swing events.

SEARCH ITEMS

Go to Search function on-line. Place quotation marks around the name of the site, select search engine, and click on "search."

"Contra Dance Links"
Extensive set of links to contra dancing pages. This is a great place to start for information on contra dance. Also, try Kiran Wagle's contra dance page, Dwayne Johnson's National Contra Dance Web Page directory, Bob Stein's "list of links by state," and Gary Shapiro's description of contra dancing.

"Henry's Dance Hotlist"
http://zeus.ncsa.uiuc.edu:8080/~hneeman/dance_hotlist.html
Extensive listing of dance pages on the Web, including swing, ballroom, Argentine tango, salsa, and C/W.

"Lindy Hop Links"
www.panix.com/~vannevar/swing.htm
Links to Lindy Hop-related internet sites.

"The New England Swing Dance Server"

www.javanet.com/~stefan/
dance/ne_swing.html
Swing dance events in both the NE area and nationally. Other dance links as well.

"US Swing Dance Server"

List of swing dance clubs and events, styles of swing dancing, dance steps, sources of videos and literature, as well as other dance links.

"Yahoo's Ballroom Dancing Index"

www.yahoo.com/arts/perform-ing_arts/dance/ballroom
Wealth of information on clubs, dances, videos.

MUSIC

Below are music samplers—a compilation of CDs and singles for some of the various dances discussed in this book. Because music can change rapidly in some forms of dance such as West Coast Swing, Retro swing, and shag, I have begun by list-ing some internet sites where you will find the most up-to-date selections. Also check the "Videotapes & Music" section in this guide. Whether old or new, this music should get your feet moving.

Dance Trax International

www.realdance.com
800-513-2623
Dedicated primarily to ball-room dance music, this site is run by Rick Popp, a profes-sional dance instructor. He rates each music track accord-ing to its suitability for dancing, on a scale of 0-5. You can search his database by rating, as well as other criteria. It also contains a recom-mended music list of what's hot and what's not.

DJ "G" Parmerton

www.musicfordancing.com/
top10/
DJ "G" Parmerton's Top 10 West Coast Swing songs.

Shag Atlanta's Shag Dance Server

www.shagatlanta.com
Club list, party calendar, shag dance instructors, membership information, and more. Also lists top 40 shag songs.
Hotline: 678-442-6457

Stefan Gonick's West Coast Swing Music Recommendations

www.javanet.com/~stefan/
dance/music.html
West Coast Swing music recommendations.

Wanna Dance Records

www.wannadance.com
Email: djmez@wannadance.com
Excellent selection of Lindy CDs, as well as WCS, shag & beach, Latin & hustle, and ballroom. Instructional videos and interactive CD-Roms are available, as well as custom CDs, dance books, clothing, acces-sories, and more. Great site.

BALLROOM

Only CDs are listed for ball-room because it is so much easier (not to mention cheaper) to buy one or two CDs than to attempt to purchase individual song titles for each of the various ballroom dances. Music by various artists may be played at different tempos, some of which are not appropriate for that dance. Ballroom CDs tend to eliminate this concern.

If you cannot find the following CDs at your local store, check the listing "Videotapes & Music" in this Resource Guide. Many of these vendors will carry most, if not all, of the CDs listed below. Dance Trax International is an especially helpful resource.

CDs:

American Opus—only CD with one song in each category to NDCA tempos. Available through Dance Trax International.

Casa Musica Collection

Claude Blouin CDs, Vol. 1-10

Giants of Latin

Gunter Noris and His Gala Orchestra

Klaus Hallen Collection

Latin Jam I, II, and III

Musica Caliente Collection

Pro Dance CDs, Vol. 1-3. Volumes 2 & 3 are the best.

Ross Mitchell Collection

SHAG

Tempo: 115-150 BPM

Songs:

"Let's Rock Awhile", Amos Milburn

"Shakin' the Shack", The Fantastic Shakers or Big John Dickerson

"Slowly", Arthur Prysock

"My Heart", The Stylistics

"Sunny Side of the Street", Frankie Laine

"Pink Champagne", Joseph Liggins

"Too Much Drink, Not Enough Sleep", The Fantastic Shakers

"Canadian Sunset", The Mills Brothers

"Honey Drippin Daddy", Joseph Liggins

"Why Fight the Feeling," Roy Hamilton

"Be Careful If You Can't Be Good", Buddy Johnson

"Over the Rainbow", Billy Williams

CDs:

Ducks 1, 2, 3, 4, 5, and 6 (Available at Judy's House of Oldies—See "Videotapes & Music")

Swing Music (Lindy, East Coast Swing, Jitterbug)
Tempo: 140-184 BPM (Some tempos will exceed this.)

Singles:

"Flying Home", Lionel Hampton & His Septet

"T'Aint What You Do", Jimmie Lunceford (or Eight-To-The-Bar)

"In The Mood", Glenn Miller & His Orchestra

"Chattanooga Choo-Choo", Glenn Miller & His Orchestra

"Little Brown Jug", Glenn Miller & His Orchestra

"Tuxedo Junction", Erskin Hawkins & His Orchestra or The Glenn Miller Orchestra

"Take the 'A' Train", Duke Ellington & His Famous Orchestra

"Jersey Bounce", Benny Goodman

"Kansas City", Jay MacShann or The Best of Claude Blouin, Vol. 2

"Choo Choo Ch'Boogie", A League of Their Own

CDs:

"Zoot Suit Riot" (Mayo Records), Cherry Poppin' Daddies

"Self-titled" (Coolsville Records), Big Bad Voodoo Daddy

"The Dirty Boogie" (Interscope), The Brian Setzer Orchestra

"Wheels Start Turning" (Ridge Records), Blues Jumpers

"Really Swingin'," Roll Up the Rug Series

The Big Bands, Vol. 1, 2, & 3, The BBC Big Band Orchestra.

WEST COAST SWING

Tempo: 110-138 BPM

"Mustang Sally", Buddy Guy or The Commitments

"The Way You Do the Things You Do", *American Opus Vol. One*

"Ability to Swing", Patti Austin

"Fannie Mae", Mambo Brothers

"Too Much Drink (Not Enough Sleep)", The Fantastic Shakers

"Bad Case Of Love", B.B. King

"Eat at Joe's" Suzy Bogguss

"All I Wanna Do", Sheryl Crow

"Fever", Elvis Presley

"The Ironic Twist", Jimmie Vaughan

CDs:

Swingin' the Blues, Vol. 1-5. If you can't find these CDs locally, they're available at CD Universe on the Web (www.cduniverse.com/asp/cdu _main.asp.)

NATIONAL ORGANIZATIONS

CDSS (Country Dance and Song Society, Inc.)
132 Main Street
P.O. Box 338
Haydenville, MA 01039
Contact: Pat MacPherson
413-268-7426
www.cdss.org
Email: sales@cdss.org
Source of information for people interested in folk-related dances such as contra dance. Members receive a bi-monthly newsletter. An annual directory, books and recordings, as well as a list of instructors are available. CDSS also organizes summer dance camps for adults and families.

National Teachers Association (NTA)
Kelly Gellette
702-735-5418

SOS (Society of Stranders)
Myrtle Beach, SC
Contact: Phil Sawyer
888-SOS-3113 (888-767-3113)
www.shagdance.com
Spring (April) and fall (September) gatherings. Social, party, and all-around good time. $35 membership includes subscription to their publication, the *Carefree Times* (four issues per year, although only two are mailed. You must pick up the others at the beach during their spring and fall gatherings. Membership also includes free admission to all participating clubs during these two events.

United Country Western Dance Council (UCWDC)
Secretary: Josie Neel
757-875-1172
www.ucwdc.org
Email: support@ucwdc.org
Governing body for over 50 events worldwide. Country western couples and line dancing. Complete list of international events.

United States Amateur Ballroom Dancers Association (USABDA)
Mary Schaufert
800-447-9047
717-235-4183
www.usabda.org
Events, magazines, local chapters (chapter directory). Youth College Network (YCN) for high school, college and university students.

World Hustle Dance Council (WHDC)
www.whdc.net
Event information, contest rules and competition winners.

World Swing Dance Council (WSDC)
Contact: Annie Hirsch
949-673-8893
Fax: 949-675-2084
www.swingdancecouncil.com
Email: WSDCannie@aol.com
Excellent list of national events, swing dance instructors, plus other recommended dance links.

PUBLICATIONS

5678 Dance Magazine
7 Park Avenue, Suite 100
Gaithersburg, MD 20877
301-216-0200
Fax: 301-869-7432
www.5678magazine.com
Email: durand5678@aol.com
$39.95/year. A full color
monthly magazine that covers
the worlds of swing, country,
Lindy, ballroom, hustle, shag,
and more. Contains articles on
dance events, technique, etc., as
well as lists of dance teachers,
major events, and associations.
Everything you need to keep
you dancing.

Amateur Dancers
Robert Meyer, Editor
1427 Gibsonwood Road
Baltimore, MD 21228-2524
800-447-9047
www.usabda.org
Email: usabdacent@aol.com
Official bi-monthly magazine
of the United States Amateur
Ballroom Dancers Association.
Free to USABDA members.
U.S.—$23/year, Canada—
$26/year.

Ballroom Dance Competition Calendar
Dr. Peter L. Collins, Editor
7-B, 220 Central Park South
New York, NY 10019
212-541-7205
Possibly the most complete list-
ing of ballroom competitions.
Note: This publication is
undergoing a change and will

only be available electronically.
The web site is under construction at this time, so check the
USABDA internet site for more
information.

Country Dance Lines Magazine
Drawer 139
Woodacre, CA 94973
Contact: Michael Hunt
415-488-0154
Fax: 415-488-4671
Email: cdl4cwdanc@aol.com
12 issues/year, $20 U.S, $45
Canada, $55 Europe.
Includes directory of C/W
dance instructors, as well as
dance step description and
evaluation of CDs for dancing
ability. Dancing hints are also
provided. Publishes books on
C/W dancing.

Dance Beat
Keith Todd, Editor
12265 S. Dixie Hwy., PMB 9
Miami, FL 33156
305-531-3087
Email:
info@www.dancebeat.com
Monthly newspaper, $35/yr. or
$20/six months.
Geared for ballroom competi-
tors.

Dance Teacher
Caitlin Sims, Managing Editor
250 W. 51st Street, Suite 420
New York, NY 10107
212-265-8890
Fax: 212-265-8908
10 issues/yr.—$24.95.
Focuses on performing arts of

ballet, jazz, tap, and ballroom
for dance teachers.

Danceweek
Dr. Charles S. Zwerling, Editor
2709 Medical Office Place
Goldsboro, NC 27534
800-441-2515
Weekly newsletter, $33/yr.
Focuses on ballroom competi-
tion and dance-related news.

Dancing USA
Michael Fitzmaurice, Editor
200 North York Road
Elmherst, IL 60126
800-290-1307
www.dancingusa.com
6 issues/year. $24.95 includes
free how-to-dance videotape.
National bi-monthly magazine
for the romance of ballroom
swing and Latin style dancing
for the social dancer.

In The Swing Magazine
Janne Anderson
9106 Balboa Avenue
San Diego, CA 92123
619-64-SWING
Http://dancers.com/janne/
magazine/magazine.html
Email: janneswing@aol.com
Quarterly publication. $35/year.
Covers West Coast Swing, retro
swing, Lindy Hop, shag, hustle,
and country western. Provides
tips and articles by leading fig-
ures in the dance community.
Also includes competition
photos and results. Also a
source of swing CDs.

Linedancer Magazine
Clare House
166 Lord Street
Southport, Merseyside
PR9 0QA
England
011-44-1704-501235
www.linedancermagazine.com
A full color monthly magazine
for line dancers. Events, fea-
tures, technique, and more.
Mostly covers England and
Europe, but expanding to
include the US and Australia.

VACATIONS
Ballroom Vermont
Box 4179
Portsmouth, NH 03801
800-242-8785
www.ballroomdancecamp.com
Email: jazvermont@aol.com

Bridge to the Tango
P.O. Box 560127
West Medford, MA 02156
888-382-6467
Fax: 617-666-4316
www.tangobridge.com/dtango7
Email: dtango7@aol.com
Specializing in the tango. Videos
and music. Also offers four
tango tours per year to various
cities such as Buenos Aires,
Paris, London, San Francisco.
Free catalog. Call between 9
a.m. and 5 p.m. for assistance.

The Cloister
Sea Island, GA 31561
800-SEA-ISLAND
www.seaisland.com
An array of annual dance festivals and events.

Cruises Plus
800-953-6050

Dancers at Sea
1625 Bethel Road, Suite 102
Columbus, OH 43220
614-527-0440
Fax: 614-451-9991
www.dancersatsea.com
Dance cruises catering to both singles and couples.

Dynamic Cruise Concepts
One Harbor Place
1901 S. Harbor City, Suite 803
Melbourne, FL 39201
888-328-5958
www.dynamiccruiseconcepts.com
Offers theme cruises such as Big Band, Legends of Rock & Roll, and much more. And, for all of you wannabe authors, they even offer a Writers Research cruise.

Mohonk Mountain Resort
1000 Mountain West Road
New Paltz, NY 12561
800-772-6646
www.mohonk.com
Offers various dance weekends each year, including swing, tango, and ballroom.

Scott's Oquaga Lake House
P.O. Box 47
Oquaga Lake
Deposit, NY 13754
607-467-3094
www.tempotek.com/cyber-town/scotts.htm
Weekend dance vacations.

Special Event Cruises
321 E Street, Suite B
Chula Vista, CA 91910
800-326-0373
www.specialeventcruises.com
A cruise agency that offers monthly Carribean vacations, including Big Band cruises.

Stardust Dance Weekends
P.O. Box 157
Woodbourne, NY 12788
800-537-2797
www.stardustdance.com
Email: stardust@catskill.net
Offers five dance weekends per year in the Catskills. Usually includes swing and ballroom music.

Stepping Out Dance Studios
1780 Broadway
New York, NY
212-245-5200
Johnny Martinez and Diane Lachtrupp
Tango dance tour. Yearly spring trip to Buenos Aires, Argentina (the Paris of South America) for tango dancers. Includes dance classes.

Swing Camp Catalina
Pasadena Dance Club
Erin and Tammy Stevens
626-799-1179 or 626-799-5689
www.swingcamp.com
Swing dance weekends.

Swingin at Sea & Country Swingin at Sea
Contact: Beata Howe
4806 Fountain Ave, # 132
Los Angeles, CA 90020
818-500-YEAH
www.dancecalendar.com/beatayeah
Email: beatayeah@aol.com

Beata organizes only a few dance cruises, and they are well attended. It is not unusual to have over 400 people of all ages, comprising both singles and couples, dancing their way across the sea.

Working Vacation
815-485-8307
www.theworkingvacation.com
For gentlemen hosts on cruises.

Zoe's Cruises and Tours
5432 Q Street
Sacramento, CA 95819
800-444-4256
Fax: 916-451-0937
www.zoescruises.com
Offers dance cruises, as well as wine and golf cruises.

VIDEOTAPES & MUSIC

A.R.B.S.P. Videos & Music
1220 Mission Canyon
Santa Barbara, CA 93105
1-888-272-7772
www.arbsp
Instructional and event videos for Lindy Hop, Swing, Shim Sham, Shag, Ballroom. T-shirts and other items available.

AMUSE-A-MOOD CO.
128 Hancock Place N.E.
Leesburg, VA 20176
703-779-8234
http://members.aol.com/
AmuseAMood/home.htm
Specializes in audio and video dance products.

Bridge to the Tango
P.O. Box 560127

West Medford, MA 02156
888-382-6467
Fax: 617-666-4316
Email: dtango7@aol.com
Specializing in the Argentine tango. Videos and music. Also offers four tango tours per year to various cities such as Buenos Aires, Paris, London, San Francisco. Free catalog. Call between 9 a.m. and 5 p.m. for assistance.

Butterfly Video
Box 184
Dept. DUSA 697
Antrum, NH 03440
800-43-DANCE
Fax: 603-588-3205
Ballroom, swing, and C/W videos.

B&M Dance Videos
3381 S. Leisure World #1A
Silver Spring, MD 20906
Email: berfield@bellatlantic.net
Ballroom videotapes for beginners and average dancers.

C. Martin Video
406 Hinsdale Lane
Silver Spring, MD 20901
301-587-7818

Charlie & Jackie Productions
1206 Dunwoody Walk
Atlanta, GA 30338
770-512-7848
Instructional videos for the Carolina Shag and WCS. Shag and swing CDs also available.

Dance Books International
4866 Dipzinski Road
Gaylord, MI 49735
Jack Henley's illustrated

ballroom dance books.

Dance Lovers USA
P.O. Box 7071
Asheville, NC 28802
1-800-FOXTROT
Complete courses on tape.
Practice music on cassettes also
available. Free brochure available.

Dance Magic
P.O. Box 851318
Richardson, TX 75085-1318
800-456-DEMO
Fax: 214-342-1969
www.dancemagic.com
Videocassettes for ballroom,
latin, C/W.

Dance Plus
2018 Granby Drive
Oakville, Ontario, L6H 3X9
Canada
888-844-4122
Fax: 905-849-4122
www.danceplus.com
Ballroom dance supply company that sells strict-time
ballroom dance CDs.

Dance Trax International
Rick Popp
2217 N. Woodbridge Street
Saginaw, MI 48602
800-513-2623
517-799-0348
Fax: 517-799-0370
www.realdance.com
Email: magnumrp@aol.com
Rick Popp is a professional
dance instructor who sells ballroom dance music and other
supplies. He rates each music
track as to its suitability for

dancing, on a scale of 0-5. To
my knowledge, he is the only
supplier to do this. He or his
staff can tell you what dance to
do to any track on a CD that
he sells.

Dance Vision
8933 West Sahara Ave.
Las Vegas, NV 89117
800-851-2813
www.dancevision.com
One-stop dance shop.
Videotapes, dance fashions,
shoes, jewelry, CDs, books,
dance camps.

Disc-Tec
Jack & Judy Hughes
P.O. Box 7595
Newark, DE 19714
302-737-7869
Email:
disctec@worldnet.att.net
Jack and Judy are DJs and
Music Coordinators for many
of the ballroom dance competitions in the U.S. They sell
dance CDs through mail order
and at competitions they
attend. Catalog available.

Dressler Enterprises-JTM
6515 East Chaparral Road
Scottsdale, AZ 85253
602-946-6360
Ballroom, West Coast Swing,
and Shag videotapes.

Everybody Dances
Elizabeth Benjamin
81 East 7th St.
New York, NY 10003
212-388-9555
Series of videotapes showcasing

various instructors in Lindy, West Coast Swing, and Shag.

Fun of Touch Dancing
3235 NE 5th St.
Pompano Beach, FL 33062
954-782-3816
Ballroom videotapes including basics, technique and styling.

Good Times Productions
P.O. Box 50928
Dept. D
Phoenix, AZ 85076-0928
800-346-8280
Polka and social dance videos.

Jim Forest Dance Instruction Videotapes
513 Gilmoure Drive
Silver Spring, MD 20901
301-593-8933
American ballroom series of videotapes plus others. Beginning to advanced levels. Free catalog available.

Judy's House of Oldies
300 Main Street
North Myrtle Beach, SC
843-249-8649
Shag music and books.

Helmut Licht's Musical Services
409 Lyman Avenue
Baltimore, MD 21212
410-323-0866
Fax: 410-433-7948
www.ballroommusic.com
Ballroom cassettes and CDs.

Living Traditions
2442 NW Market Street, #168
Seattle, WA 98107
800-500-2364 or 206-781-1238

Fax: 206-781-8733
www.ltdance.com
Email: ltdance@nwlink.com
Videos and CDs geared specifically toward swing dancing.

PRODANCE
Tom and Juliana DelFlore
P.O. Box 272822
Boca Raton, FL 33427-2822
800-992-9282 or 561-243-9382
Fax: 561-243-1002
www.prodance.com

SavoyStyle Swing Dance Shop
32101 Ellison Way
Fort Bragg, CA 95437
888-507-2869
Fax: 707-964-4473
www.swingdanceshop.com
Email: swing@savoystyle.com
Swing dance videos and CDs.

See-Do Productions
Michael Miller
P.O. Box 135
Croton-on-Hudson, NY 10520
914-271-3806
Ballroom dance videos and CDs. Exclusive Blackpool videos.

Skippy Blair Productions
10804 Woodruff Avenue
Downey, CA 90241
562-869-8949
Fax: 562-862-7129
www.skippyblair.com
Email: skippyuus@aol.com
Excellent source of West Coast Swing videos and books. Skippy's beginner and intermediate level West Coast Swing video is one of the few that emphasize timing and phrasing,

making it a great training tape.

SODANCEABIT
800-64-DANCE
Award-winning videos. Learn to dance and keep fit. Free catalog available.

Tanguero Productions
5351 Corteen Place
North Hollywood, CA 91607
323-930-1244
http://home.earthlink.net/
~tanguero/
Email: tanguero@earthlink.net
Instructional videos for beginners and intermediates.

Telemark Dance Records
Richard Mason
P.O. Box 55
McLean, VA 22101
703-450-7760
Dick Mason is the editor of the Potomac Ballroom Dance News. He sells dance CDs, videos, and books.

Wanna Dance Records
888-938-4700
www.wannadance.com
Email:
djmez@wannadance.com
Excellent selection of Lindy CDs, as well as WCS, shag & beach, latin & hustle, and ballroom. Instructional videos and interactive CD-Roms are available, as well as custom CDs, dance books, clothing, accessories, and more. Great site.

WorldTone Music, Inc.
230 Seventh Avenue, 2nd floor
New York, NY 10011

212-691-1934
Dance CDs, videos, shoes, and audio equipment. They carry hard-to-find ballroom recordings that may not be available anywhere else.

MISCELLANEOUS

Arthur Murray International, Inc.
1077 Ponce De Leon Blvd.
Coral Gables, FL 33134
305-445-9645
Fax: 305-445-0451
www.ArthurMurray.com

Fred Astaire Dance Studios
7900 Glades Road, Suite 630
Boca Raton, FL 33434
561-218-3237
Fax: 561-218-3299
www.FredAstaire.com
Email: dance@fads.com

Association of Carolina Shag Clubs
Contact: Mike Rank
704-892-1114
www.shagdance
Umbrella organization of approximately 100 shag clubs.

Golden State Dance Teachers Association
10804 Woodruff Avenue
Downey, CA 90241
562-869-8949
Fax: 562-862-7129
www.skippyblair.com
Email: skippyuus@aol.com
Provides training for teachers, students, and judges.

NATIONAL SWING DANCE EVENTS

Courtesy of the World Swing Dance Council
http://www.swingdancecouncil.com/

January

Monterey Swingfest
Monterey, CA
805-937-1574
ccsd@thegrid.net

February

Capitol SDC Convention
Sacramento, CA
916-422-5801
grmqzaz@juno.com

Jitterbug Jam
Thousand Oaks, CA
805-643-3114
www.modancin.com

March

March Madness
East Coast
313-869-9385
PauletteBrockington@yahoo.com

Boston Tea Party
Boston, MA
617-254-8700
djmez@wannadance.com

April

North Atlantic Dance Championships
Meadowlands, NJ
860-242-6803
dancepros@cyberzone.net

Seattle's Easter Swing
Seattle, WA
425-774-9662

sesdance@aol.com /
seattlewcswing.com

Texas Classic Swing Dance
Dallas, TX
817-654-1736
startext.net/homes/classic/
index.htm

American Lindy Hop Championships
East Coast
313-869-9385
PauletteBrockington@yahoo.com

May

Chicago Classic
Chicago, IL
773-202-1823
Yantonacci@aol.com

Swing Break
Santa Clara, CA
707-544-8184
swingbreak.com

Fresno Classic
Fresno, CA
559-486-1556
szener@psnw.com

Grand National Dance Championship
Atlanta, GA
770-512-7848
charlieandjackie.com

June

Jack & Jill O'Rama
Newport Beach, CA
800-537-8937
Justswing@webtv.net

Summer Dance Camp
Woodland Hills, CA
805-529-8241
Jaybdancer@aol.com

Swing by the Sea
Thousand Oaks, CA
805-937-1574
ccsd@thegrid.net

July

Phoenix July 4th Convention
Scottsdale, AZ
800-598-2538
www.amug.org/~gpsdc/ctigges
@home.com

Sundance Summer Dance Festival
Palm Springs, CA
714-99-DANCE
Sundance-Dance-Club.com

Swing & Country in Laughlin
Laughlin, NV
310-530-0500
www.dancefun.com

West Coast S State Championships
Sacramento, CA
619-272-5933
Wcssc@the-voter.com
(Lloyd@the-voter.com)

August

Beale Street Party
Memphis, TN
901-755-1269
jegan@midsouth.rr.com

Washington DC Swing Fling
Virginia
505-286-8646
durand5678@aol.com

Swingtime in the Rockies
Denver, CO
303-696-7743
dance@letsdancedenver.com

Michigan Dance Classic
Mt. Pleasant, MI
810-694-7625
Bbudzyn@tir.com

Summer Hummer
Stamford, CT
860-242-6803
dancepros@cyberzone.net

September

Dallas D.A.N.C.E.
Dallas, TX
214-526-8889
www.dallasdance.com

California Boogie and Blues
Long Beach, CA
310-530-0500
www.dancefun.com

Northwest Swing Dance Championships
Spokane, WA
509-468-8342
bobking1@webtv.net

Virginia State Open Championships
Virginia
703-698-9811
potomacswing.com/vso

October

American Lindy Hop Championships
East Coast
313-869-9385
paulettebrockington@yahoo.com

Boogie by the Bay TNGSDC
San Francisco, CA
415-979-4456
tngsdc.org/boogie.html

Halloween Swingthing
Thousand Oaks, CA
805-937-1574
ccsd@thegrid.net

November

Mountain Magic
North Lake Tahoe, CA
415-585-6282
wcdancer@ix.netcom.com

Swingin' New England Dance Festival
MA
617-527-9464
nklein@lesley.edu

US Open SD Championships
Century City, CA
800-537-8937
Justswing@webtv.net

December

New Years Dance Camp
Bakersfield, CA
805-529-8241
Jaybdancer@aol.com

New Years Dance Extravaganza
Boston, MA
860-242-6803
dancepros@cyberzone.net

New Years Swing Dance Classic
Fresno, CA
559-486-1556
szener@psnw.com

FURTHER READING
Dance
Allen, Jeff, *Quickstart to Social Dancing* (QQS Publications, 1998)

Blair, Skippy, *Dance Power, Own the Experience* (Skippy Blair Publications, 1998)

Blair, Skippy, *Disco to Tango and Back* (Skippy Blair Publications, 1978)

Bottomer, Paul, *Let's Dance* (Anness Publishing Limited, 1998)

Pener, Degen, *The Swing Book* (Back Bay Books, 1999)

Reynolds, John Lawrence, *Ballroom Dancing: The Romance, Rhythm and Style* (Laurel Glen Publishing, 1998)

Stearns, Marshall & Jean, *Jazz Dance* (Da Capo Press, 1994)

Vale, V., *Swing! The New Retro Renaissance* (V/Search Publications, 1998)

Relationships
Dominitz, Ben, *How to Find the Love of Your Life* (Prima Publishing, 1994)

Godek, Gregory J.P., *1001 Ways To Be Romantic* (Casa Blanca Press, 1993)

Lowndes, Leil, *How to Make Anyone Fall in Love with You* (Contemporary Books, 1995)

Ratcliff, Roger, *How to Meet the Right Man* (Carol Publishing Group, 1996)

Ratcliff, Roger, *How to Meet the Right Woman* (Carol Publishing Group, 1996)

Wolf, Sharyn, *Guerrilla Dating Tactics* (Plume, 1994)

Give the gift of *Three Minutes of Intimacy* to your loved ones, friends, and colleagues

Quick Order Form

Yes, I want _____ copies of *Three Minutes of Intimacy* at $12.95 each, plus $4 shipping for the first book and $2 for each additional copy. (New York residents please add 8.25% sales tax per book.) International orders: $9 for first book; $5 for each additional copy (estimate).

My check or money order for $_____ is enclosed. I understand that I may return any book(s) ordered for a full refund—for any reason, no questions asked.

Please charge my ☐ Visa ☐ Matercard

Name_____

Organization _____

Address _____

City/State/Zip _____

Phone _____Email _____

Card # _____Exp. date _____

Signature _____

Please make your check payable and return to:

Sundance Publishing Inc.
P.O. Box 932
Patchogue, NY 11772

Phone your credit card order to: 888-203-5862
Fax your order to: 631-289-3004. Send this form.
Email: orders@Sundancepublishing.net